SPIRIT GEMS

Books by Glyn Edwards and Santoshan (Stephen Wollaston):

Glyn Edwards, compiled and with an introduction by Santoshan
The Potential of Mediumship: A Collection of Essential Teachings and Exercises

Glyn Edwards and Santoshan, with a foreword by Don Hills
The Spirit World in Plain English: Mediumistic and Spiritual Unfoldment
(revised and updated edition of *Tune in to your Spiritual Potential*)

Santoshan, with conversations with Glyn Edwards
Realms of Wondrous Gifts: Psychic, Mediumistic and Miraculous Powers in the Great Mystical and Wisdom Traditions (revised eBook edition available)

Santoshan
Rivers of Green Wisdom: Exploring Christian and Yogic Earth Centred Spirituality
(GreenSpirit eBook Series)

Santoshan, with a foreword by Ian Mowll
Spirituality Unveiled: Awakening to Creative Life

Santoshan with Swami Dharmananda and a foreword by Glyn Edwards
The House of Wisdom: Yoga Spirituality of the East and West

Spirit Gems

Glyn Edwards
& Santoshan

Essential Guidance for Spiritual, Mediumistic and Creative Unfoldment

Published by
S. Wollaston, 2011
Publishing address: 11 Coronation Cottages, Akely, Bucks MK18 5HN
Note: books cannot be ordered from the above address

For Retail Orders and Wholesale Information Contact:
Mind-Body-Spirit
Telephone: (01202) 267684 / International: +441202 267684
Email: info@mindbodyspirit-uk.com
Website: www.mindbodyspiritonline.co.uk

Copyright © 2011 Glyn Edwards and Santoshan (Stephen Wollaston)

ISBN: 978-0-9569210-1-7

A CIP record of this book is available from the British Library

Spirit Gems is a revised and expanded edition of
Unleash your Spiritual Power and Grow,
a previously published 2nd edition released by Quantum,
an imprint of W Foulsham, in 2007.
The 1st edition was published under the title
21 Steps to Reach your Spirit by Quantum in 2001

The rights of Glyn Edwards and Santoshan (Stephen Wollaston) as authors have
been asserted in accordance with the Copyright, Designs and Patents Act 1988

Design and artwork: Santoshan (Stephen Wollaston)
Cover image: © Pertusinas/shutterstock.com

Printed and bound by CPI Group (UK), Croydon, CR0 4YY

Printed on FSC accredited paper

Contents

Dedicated to all students and teachers seeking to embrace a universal, all-inclusive spirituality.

Foreword to New Edition

The true Self is all-loving,
compassionate and understanding,
and dwells in the hearts of all.
– SANTOSHAN

This book could not have come into being without the help of coauthor Santoshan who thought of following the first title we did together with a more reflective and multi-faceted embrace of numerous essential realms of unfoldment. On its release it quickly out-sold our first book and became one world renowned centre's best seller, though our first book, which has since been revised and retitled, also achieved this at The Arthur Findlay College. The book has appealed greatly to different types of seekers looking for ways to include many areas explored within the text. Even the inclusion of various quotations for the last section has become something people tell us they appreciate and find useful. One reader who was once married to a known metaphysical philosopher herself wrote saying how she had taken just this one book with her whilst undergoing treatment for cancer and mentioned how it helped her through this difficult time.

In revisiting these pages for this revised and extended edition I was surprised how detailed, broad and inclusive we had been in our writing. Santoshan's diagrams are also incredibly helpful. The principle changes made have been more in the area of additional material rather than changing the contents, though we have reworked the introduction with some fresh insights. Santoshan once said he would like to be remembered for this book more than any other and I can understand why, as there is much here that goes to the heart of spiritual, mediumistic and creative fields of growth, is universal, relevant to today's life and needs to be considered in unfoldment, in our inner quests and communion with the spirit and our interactions with the natural world and others. I hope readers enjoy this new edition and will continue to find within the following sections some nourishment for their spiritual journeys.

– GLYN EDWARDS.

About the Authors

*G*lyn Edwards is internationally recognized as one of the UK's greatest mediums and teachers of spiritual and psychic science. At sixteen he joined a Benedictine community. He later became a protégée of the medium, Gordon M Higginson, and founded The Gordon Higginson Fellowship. He has been a regular and highly popular senior course tutor at the esteemed Arthur Findlay College for over three decades and has run workshops and demonstrated his mediumship throughout the world. He is a certificate holder of the Spiritualist' National Union, has coauthored books, recorded various teaching CDs and cassettes and was given the name Devadasa (servant of God) by Swami Dharmananda Saraswati Maharaj. He is particularly known for the quality of his teaching and his ability to demonstrate his mediumship almost effortlessly in front of large audiences.

*S*antoshan (Stephen Wollaston) has served as a council member of GreenSpirit, is a member of their editorial and publishing team and the designer of GreenSpirit Magazine. He was given the name Santoshan (contentment) by Swami Dharmananda and has a creative background as a writer, graphic designer, artist and musician. He was the bass guitarist of one of London's first punk rock bands, The Wasps, and is the author and coauthor of several acclaimed books, including *Spirituality Unveiled: Awakening to Creative Life* and *The House of Wisdom: Yoga Spirituality of the East and West* (coauthored). He holds a degree in religious studies and a post graduate certificate in religious education from King's College London and studied psychosynthesis psychology. He also helped to establish The Gordon Higginson Fellowship with Glyn Edwards and has a deep interest in creative, yogic and Nature centred spiritualities.

Preface

This book has been put together for the purpose of reflection and meditation. Parts One and Two consist of practical guidance for creative living, understanding spiritual laws and enhancing our spiritual gifts and potential. The teachings in these parts relate to the authentic nature of our being, to the spirit world that is both within and all around us, to daily life practices and point the way forward for all who are earnest in their search to become greater instruments for good on our beautiful planet Earth.

The two sets of twenty-one steps and their commentaries are condensed overviews of various interconnected areas of development. Readers will benefit more by absorbing just one, two or three steps at a time (not necessarily in any particular order as unfoldment is more of a spiral danced than a linear progression from one place to another) and unpacking their meaning and relevance to his or her life. Exercises are mentioned in various places and included in sections of their own. Yet reflecting upon any individual point and seeing what thoughts, insights or feelings arise is an exercise in itself.

The first set of steps focuses upon groundwork that invariably needs to be done and frequently returned to, whereas the second brings in other areas, such as awakening to our own spirit and to mediumistic awareness and their relation to the creativity of the Divine in all. The Introduction will help readers to understand how various areas mentioned in the steps relate to one another. The Questions and Answers section brings in other related topics. The last part of the book includes a variety of quotations from different teachers and disciplines, which has been included because of the richness of wisdom and understanding of spirituality that exists in various traditions.

Introduction

$\mathcal{D}$eep within each of us is the wish for peace, happiness and freedom from everyday entanglements. The search for this can be traced back hundreds of years. Some aspects, stages and views about unfoldment and various levels of awareness are almost universal.

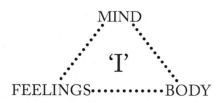

DIAGRAM 1:
Average Field of Awareness

The 'I' (our individual sense of self), the body (including the physical senses), feelings and the mind (perceptual, thinking and reasoning abilities).

The diagram above and the one at the top of the next page show the average field of awareness, the connections and interaction of various levels and ways to the true spirit Self. There are numerous degrees of awareness within each category. No clear boundary exists between them as they all work in relation to one another. Most of the time our awareness is focused around a limited area (see diagram 1) and often on a fairly superficial level. Meaning there are various levels that are often ignored. There are some that are completely unconscious, such as the actual physical processing of sensory information that happens before things enter the field of our conscious awareness.

We can become enwrapped in self-centred concerns and worldly experience and believe that this is all there is to life, even though we may be using or drawing upon other parts of our being. We might for instance use intuitive knowledge, but not be aware of doing so. We

Diagram 2: *Interconnected Paths and Levels of Awareness.*

all possess intuition. It is an essential part of spiritual unfoldment, as well as creative and mediumistic types of activity and can be experienced on a mental, emotional or physical level, such as knowing, feeling or physically experiencing something to be right or wrong. Yet an imbalance can be caused by a predominance of intuition if it is developed at the expense of other areas. Just as a predominance of the intellect, emotions or physical parts of our being would cause disharmony. This is why the lines are dotted in diagram 1; for we can become disconnected and out of balance with different areas of ourselves. All levels of our being need to be healthily in touch and in tune with one another.

It is our individual sense of 'I', our individual sense of self, that often restricts us. Yet there are many levels that are constantly open to us, and through realising wider fields of awareness we can get in touch with them (see diagram 2). Through individual, social, creative and spiritual development we open up to greater possibilities and allow all levels of our being to interact in less inhibited ways. A holistic approach will involve harmonising every part to form a more integrated and balanced whole, including a healthy understanding of our individual sense of self.

The body: sensations, automatic functions and connections with all

Everything is interconnected and is a part of us and we are a part of everyone and everything. Our physical bodies are made from the same material that once made stars, plants and other life in the universe.

The body is closely connected with our feelings, emotions and perceptions. When it is not functioning properly, our emotional and mental well-being is often affected; just as our emotional and mental states affect our bodies. It is for this reason that maintaining a healthy physical body is important in spiritual unfoldment as it can affect the ways we act and respond to life.

If we do not have awareness of our body and the body's senses, we will not be fully conscious and awake to life. We might eat food without tasting it or look at something happening without mentally registering it. An essential on-going aspect of unfoldment is to open to our senses, to become more aware of all that we experience and become creatively and actively involved in life. This does not mean that we over-indulge or become over attached to our physical senses. Here it should be noted that awareness is a state of being we often slip in and out of, generally without noticing it. Strictly speaking, we do not actually develop awareness. It is the ability of noticing whether we are aware or not that is developed, which is done by an act of will and conscious thought. This could be described as 'being observant of awareness', or paradoxically as 'being aware of awareness'. In the last description, the first type of awareness is more of a practice that can be cultivated. The latter is not something we develop, but a natural state of being we all possess. However, the more proficient we are at noticing whether we are aware or not, the greater our awareness will be.

Our bodies possess various machine-like abilities (controlled by the autonomic nervous system) that are essential for everyday living, such as heartbeat, digestive system and respiration. The way we move our bodies is often done automatically and unconsciously via various instructions from the brain, and on the whole helps us function efficiently on a physical level. When we experience something through the body's senses, the mind comes into play, draws upon stored knowledge and decides what it is we are perceiving. The thinking part of ourselves will appraise, consciously or unconsciously, whether something is pleasant or desirable or not, and then creates an emotional response that also affects our mental state. Yet we sometimes act emotionally or impulsively, as seen in the fight-or-flight response. Although impulsive actions can have positive use in some situations, they can also cause a form of emotional flooding when we allow ourselves to react unskilfully before thinking something through.

An important part of unfoldment in many traditions is to maintain a degree of awareness of our body's abilities and sensations as well as some of our daily life actions, desires, feelings and perceptions. This brings a degree of mindfulness into activity. Breath awareness is particularly important as it not only helps us to centre and calm our thoughts and bodies, but also energizes the mind and body, and helps us to be more alert and receptive for activities such as creative work and meditation practice. Walking meditation (a popular Buddhist practice) also helps us to become more mindful. The purpose behind it is to increase our level of awareness and have more influence over various physical and mental actions. Other practices, such as Hatha Yoga postures and Tai Chi, also promote awareness of the body's movements, through which we can become sensitive to certain energies (*prana* and *chi* energies) and are ways of opening up to other levels of our being and entering states of active and effortless concentration. Those who are clairvoyant also tell us that it is around the area of the body that etheric energy can be seen, which is said to be connected with the physical body and its workings.

Feelings: responses to senses and perceptions

Some misunderstand unfoldment and think it is about being emotionally disconnected, or aloof and separate from life. When sincerely embraced we discover that it entails letting life in, being in touch with our feelings, integrating various parts and not being thrown off balance by destructive emotional levels of our being.

The more aware we are of our feelings and emotions, the more open we will be to development. In the process of healthy unfoldment we need to recognize and work with our feelings and emotions and understand various things about the way we work, i.e. what motivates us, gives us pleasure, helps us to be more mindful or causes emotional upsets.

Just as our bodies possess various automatic skills, much of our emotions are spontaneous and are fed by a combination of perceptual impressions and by stored knowledge, memories and experiences. In order to find more peace in the present moment and experience life as it is without imposing any unfair judgements we will need to work on any impressions that cause us to react and stop us from being open to life. We may have to look at our environments, lifestyles, friendships, past experiences, views and beliefs and see how these are influencing us.

People who take a devotional approach to spirituality will obviously draw heavily on emotional levels of themselves. But without the cultivation of a deep compassion for all and a healthy development of the mind and the intellect there can be a danger of becoming irrational and restrictive in both our views and beliefs.

'I': our individual sense of self

This level is often associated with the small or ego self, particularly in Eastern traditions, and should not be confused with higher 'I' conscious states, which are sometimes described as ultimate levels of being. Although much of our everyday consciousness works around our individual levels of awareness, it can of course be widened to embrace other parts of our nature. An unhealthy understanding of our individual sense of self will over-feed narrow, self-centred interests that will isolate us from wider realms of life and others. On the one hand *some* Eastern traditions seem to believe that our individual sense of 'I' should be completely overcome. On the other, some Western schools of spirituality believe it can be expanded to include more than just selfish concerns. After all, we live on Earth with an individual sense of self and have duties and obligations that are connected to this awareness of ourselves. The popular spiritual psychology, Psychosynthesis, advocates being conscious of our unique individuality in order to be aware of any personal needs or issues connected to this level of ourselves.

Spiritual seekers can sometimes experience problems as they begin to widen and transform their individual awareness in order to awaken to higher states of consciousness. Two seemingly conflicting poles of interest can cause inner turmoil as we shift our perspectives from things with which we previously identified. We may experience insecurity as

15

old patterns of thought, beliefs or behaviour are changed. It can be a difficult stage of unfoldment – a time of trial before a new life is firmly established. Determination is often needed to work with any insights we have and to overcome any problems, as this helps us to awaken to our inherent natural wisdom and our spiritual will and establish a healthy level of self-mastery, as well as stability and confidence in our life's direction.

Conceptions (the intellect) and perceptions

Perceptions are not a *direct* link to the senses. Information is turned into neural signals and analysed by various channels that generate an explanation of what we are sensing. Yet even our slightest perceptions are highly influenced by our stored knowledge. We each create our own interpretations of the world, which are based on what we know and have experienced. Yogic traditions have long held notions about the potential behind every situation sowing seeds in our unconscious minds that affect our interpretations of life. It is by awakening to deep intuitive knowledge, wise discernment and compassion that new and more healthier patterns are created and unhelpful beliefs and perceptions are transformed.

Our conceptual, intellectual or rational mind is sometimes seen by mystical and spiritual schools of development as inferior and a barrier to intuition as it can sometimes inhibit its flow. Yet it is an essential part of who we are and if used beneficially it can help us to express inspiration and spiritual knowledge in more structured and dynamic ways. If we wish to follow spiritual paths, we will need to be aware of how this level affects our judgements and views and learn how to use it creatively. Various types of meditation practice can help us achieve this by slowing down our continuous stream of thoughts, giving us the opportunity to observe how we work psychologically and spiritually and discover how we can open ourselves to positive and creative qualities of our true nature. This will often require bringing in an element of nonattachment (not being bound by inhibiting conditions) and mindfulness in order to open our minds to other realms of consciousness and transform any restrictive patterns.

The way to use this level to our advantage is to cultivate higher reasoning, wholesome views – such as a respect for all life – flexibility of thought, openness to new ideas and experience, to analyse, know and accept ourselves and others and see how we can develop and grow further, and be more compassionate, caring and loving. By fine tuning our views and perceptions we can also open up more to the following levels.

Levels of mindfulness (the observer), insight and intuitive awareness

Mindfulness, insight and intuitive awareness are abilities that can work together or separately and help us to progress further onto other paths of experience and being. Mindfulness works in two ways: it helps us to become more aware of our everyday thoughts, feelings and actions and opens us to other essential parts of ourselves. It focuses the mind, nourishes understanding and helps us observe our minds, bodies, feelings and emotions in order to see how they affect us and can be harmonised with one another. Additionally, mindfulness supplies us with the power to disidentify (the ability of being aware of and in touch with different parts of ourselves and conscious that we are much more than them) from realms solely connected with the mind, body and emotions and awaken to wider spheres of awareness. Insight and intuitive awareness can also help us understand our psychological and spiritual nature and change unbeneficial patterns of thought or behaviour. They are crucial abilities for numerous areas of unfoldment, such as psychic, creative, mediumistic and spiritual development.

Various spiritual traditions view mindfulness, insight and intuition as higher functions of the mind. Though a developed intuitive faculty does not always indicate spiritual growth as it can function on many levels and will depend on how it is used and affects our lives. It is through the creative use of these three abilities that we start to look deeply into ourselves and awaken to qualities of our true spirit nature. Yet the path that leads to it includes a realm that has been documented by many spiritual and mystical traditions (described under the following heading).

Creative and psychic activity

Every tradition has a different interpretation of this level, how it functions and what it does. Basically it consists of creative and psychic energy or power and is a universal force that is said to exist and be active in all life in the universe. Modern science also tells us that the cosmos is a sea of energy.

Tantric Yoga connects this level with the Goddess and her creative power. In the book *Natural Grace*, Cambridge biologist Rupert Sheldrake found similarities with this notion and ideas about Mother Nature, Gaia (the Earth as a living organism) and his own theories concerning the psychic nature of life, which shares some similarities with Carl Jung's collective unconscious.

This level is the realm of inspiration, creativity, universal cosmic consciousness, spiritual awakening and mystical and psychic activity. It is open to us all via our intuitive abilities and its influence can be experienced intellectually, emotionally or physically. In some cases, opening to this level can be unpredictable and is why guidance is sometimes needed from an experienced teacher who possesses knowledge and practical understanding of various stages of unfoldment. For some the path to their true spirit nature is gentle and gradual, whereas others can find it littered with sudden and difficult openings that throw their emotional and mental lives into periods of spiritual crises as they open to things with which they are unfamiliar. Some may even experience physical ailments as changes are brought about, which can be due to stress and emotional wounds being released. Even if this is so, medical advice must always be sought.

All kinds of experiences have been documented by those who have opened widely to this level, such as visions, hearing spirit voices, out-of-body experiences, seeing psychic lights and so on. Though often seen as signs of progress on spiritual paths, if the groundwork has not been done these experiences can be problematic for some students who are not used to them. So care, common sense and a reliable network of supportive, understanding friends and knowledgeable helpers are things worth considering.

Some artists and poets appear to be inspired by the spiritual aspect of this level. Of particular interest is the work of William Wordsworth, as well as reports of various other Nature mystics, who experienced the world as vividly alive and permeated by a Divine presence. It is also at this level that people have encounters with individual spirit personalities and archetypes (universal mental symbols).

When we focus and energize our mind and body through spiritual exercises, we draw power from this level and begin to transform and refine our levels of being and our spiritual understanding. Yet this is not the final stage or goal of unfoldment. Traditions of both the East and West have for many years recognized levels beyond it, where mystics, of which we all have the potential to be, discover profound insights into their true nature, and many sometimes speak of stages of struggle before fully awakening to it, where we are invited to go deeper into ourselves.

There can of course be various difficult stages on spiritual paths. One that often precedes a more open awareness of the following realm can be a stage where uplifting experiences in our spiritual growth are absent and the centre of our psychological being is transformed more than before. Only patience, perseverance and the realisation that such times of growth are beneficial and will leave us spiritually stronger, seem to help earnest travellers accept and evolve through these important life changing periods in their unfoldment.

Spirit/authentic Self

It should be noted that various writers have different interpretations of this level and use a variety of terms to describe what they see as an ultimate stage of being and understanding. Though it ought to be mentioned that spiritual growth does not stop here, but still continues and spills over into and becomes an essential part of regular daily life, and will influence spiritual awareness and conduct. It is often seen as a state of internalised awareness that leads to supreme insight into our nature and connecting deeply with all. Through it we attain profound knowledge of our authentic spirit Selves and our relationship with everything and everyone. Different terms used for this realm are the transpersonal, real or higher Self. Buddhists mention a state of selflessness and realising our pure Buddha nature. These higher planes of awareness are sometimes described as the levels of 'I', 'unitive' or 'pure' (unconditioned) consciousness, where the distinction between subject and object – experiencer and experienced – merges into one non-separate reality. Because this level is so different from ordinary conceptual awareness, many find it hard to describe and often prefer to say what it is not rather than what it is, as nothing that can be named truly describes it (which is all a part of its mystery). Yet it invariably brings about stability and a sense of wholeness and living in the world without being inhibited by trivial everyday entanglements of life.

Here we realise the connectedness of all life, discover a transcendent reality behind everyday experience and recognize the creative Divinity of all (which obviously links deeply with the previous heading). It is often characterised by qualities of good, love, compassion, peace and wisdom and experienced as a level of pure awareness, pure bliss and pure being. Because this level interacts with all others, there are numerous states and stages of awakening to it, as well as various experiences associated with it. If you are interested in knowing more about different traditional paths and what they see as final points of freedom you will find Daniel Goleman's *The Meditative Mind* a helpful introduction.

The following two sets of steps cover various areas of unfoldment that relate to these different levels of ourselves. Our previous book *The Spirit World in Plain English* also explains various aspects of our being in a chapter on the human aura.

Our true nature is forever trying
to awaken us to how we can be;
all we have to do is listen.

Part 1

Twenty-one Steps to
Openness and Freedom

Commentary by Santoshan

*O*penness is an essential ingredient of spiritual unfoldment. It encompasses freedom from past conditioning and everyday entanglements, allowing our hearts to open, healing our wounds, discovering what is inherent within us, finding our true spiritual nature, and embracing and connecting more deeply with ourselves, others and the vast ocean of life that surrounds us. It is an inner journey that leads to resolving conflicts, developing the will, awakening to beauty and compassion and manifesting creative and intuitive powers. But there is no actual point where a traveller can say he or she has arrived at the journey's end, as the search is a continual and ever-evolving process in which there are many awakenings and openings along the way.

The American writer and spiritual teacher, Jack Kornfield, sensibly described spirituality in the following way:

> *In the beginning we may erroneously imagine spiritual practice to be a linear journey, travelling over a certain landscape to a faraway destination of enlightenment. But it is better described as a widening circle or spiral that opens our hearts and gradually infuses our consciousness to include all of life as a spiritual whole.*[1]

Openness is something that constantly needs to be checked and reassessed. In order to achieve and handle it healthily we will need to learn a certain amount of skill in unfolding it. In the early stages we may find there are times when opening is difficult because it makes us more sensitive to our emotions and environments before we are fully ready to understand, accept and respond creatively to what is going on within and around us. This may cause us to withdraw and believe life is safer when we are closed down than attempting to connect more with our feelings, needs and environments, as well as those with whom we live and work.

In the process of opening ourselves there can be various growing as well as disheartening experiences like this. They may make us feel emotionally raw and vulnerable, or as though we have failed or made a false start. But we should realise we have taken an important step and learned something about where we are now and how we currently respond to and feel about life, or certain issues or situations. This is all a part of what the search for growth is about. It demonstrates that openness is not necessarily easy, and that even when achieved we still have to be aware of what is going on at various levels of our being and understand why we may find openness difficult to sustain at times.

For many it can be hard to maintain and be problematic until they are more prepared and stronger in their unfoldment. For example, if we live or work with someone who drains our energy or unsettles our emotions, it would be wise to resolve such problems before opening to more sensitive areas within ourselves. We must remember that we have to honour and take care of our own well-being in order to live healthily on a daily basis.

There is nothing wrong with closing down occasionally as it is a natural defence mechanism that can help to protect us in times of trouble. But we need to be conscious of when we are doing it and why and realise that being continuously defensive is a sign of insecurity. We will need to be aware of closing down unnecessarily, as it can cause us to miss out on experiencing and discovering much more to life as well as developing and growing further.

The following steps and commentary can be viewed as covering three areas connected with the subject of openness and ways of finding spiritual freedom in everyday life:

1. Beginning the search and finding traces.

2. Obstacles along the way.

3. Awakening to qualities of our authentic nature.

1. Have respect for all spiritual traditions – any belief, practice or philosophy that helps humankind to become more open, caring and compassionate.

Any belief, practice or philosophy that encourages and embraces openness, equality and unity deserves respect. If we are prepared to look for good and the variety of ways that our true spirit Self manifests and expresses itself, we will overcome barriers between us and others. This will lead us to discover more spiritual truths and harmony with humanity and the natural world around us. Most tried and tested spiritual traditions have great value and show ways in which we can be more deeply in touch with and manifest our true nature.

There are many paths that have been used to awaken individuals to their true Selves and free them from limiting conditions, such as the path of selfless work and service for others, the path of insight and knowledge and the path of devotion to the Divine in all. It is debatable whether these can be practised in total isolation from one another. For we cannot love God unless we have a certain amount of knowledge of God's ways. Similarly, we cannot perform good deeds unless we have a certain amount of compassion and love for others. A holistic approach involves healthily integrating all levels of body, feelings, mind and spirit.

2. Develop honour, respect and reverence for all life and regard all people equally.

Many people's lives are hard, which may determine the way they are and how they act. To judge another without realising this can display a lack of understanding on our behalf.

On a visit to the British Museum I once witnessed a young boy of around three years old run into a roped-off area that contained the fourth century Hinton St Mary Mosaic Pavement. It depicts the earliest representation of Jesus yet to be found in England. It obviously has great historic value. Yet here was a young child walking all over it, possibly causing irreparable damage.

The boy's mother had not been paying attention to what her son was doing, as would be expected in such a place and seemed preoccupied. By the time she realised what had happened, it was too late to do anything about it as it would have meant her walking on the mosaic as well. The mother promptly called the boy, who came running to her with a cheeky and beaming smile on his face. Unfortunately one of the museum's guards was not so amused and sharply asked the mother to keep more of a check on her child. She immediately apologized for being distracted and mentioned receiving some worrying news that morning. The woman was clearly distressed and distracted by something.

One can only speculate how grave the news may have been, but it explains why the mother was preoccupied. The guard then seemed to realise he had over reacted – after all, we need eyes everywhere when looking after young children – and began to display some understanding for the situation. The guard himself may also have been experiencing a particularly rough day and held responsible for any damage done to the exhibit. As small as this event was, it demonstrates that the reality of a situation can be much greater than initially perceived. We therefore need to develop some patience and a wider understanding of and respect for all people and not be too quick to judge others by their actions, no matter how small or great an incident may be. This includes honouring and respecting ourselves and not being too judgemental about our own weaknesses.

The way to transform our short comings into good is first to acknowledge them, then accept and use our insights into them to awaken compassion for ourselves and others. This includes cultivating kindness, friendliness and humility, as well as honour and reverence for all – both human and non-human species. For every living thing and person has the self-same sacred spark of life within. The creatures of the world's jungles and the African plains, the living Earth beneath our feet all share an interdependent relationship with our being, just as much as we share an interdependent relationship with them. All life is interconnected with an underlying Divine unity, which is forever in the act of creating and evolving.

3. Live your life to the best of your abilities and accept the lives of others.

Spiritual growth is about coming to terms with who and what we are, understanding our inner nature and the ways in which we work:

physically, emotionally, mentally, psychically and spiritually. It means discovering our potentials – how to develop and use them to become greater instruments for good in the world. It is a path that is more accepting and does not expect things to happen or people to behave in a manner that we desire, but concentrates on how we can best develop, how we can transform, transcend, find creative solutions to and grow beyond problems that may confront us and live less complex lives.

If we examine our perceptions and judgements, we will find that they are often the products of habit, ingrained views and emotions and serve little purpose in balancing our daily lives with spiritual living. It is here that we need to begin our work and discover ways in which we can change any restrictive patterns and awaken to finer qualities within us.

4. Be receptive and open to the present and the eternal now of life.

The past has gone and only exists in our memories. There is nothing we can do that can physically change it. If we hold onto the past we will not be open to experiencing anything new. This does not mean we should deny or not learn from it. By being aware of how past events and experiences affect us, we can change the way we view them and make the present a time for growth, healing and healthy transformations.

We need to be aware that all areas of our lives have to be continually worked on and reassessed at various stages in our unfoldment, as the path to wholeness and health is about bringing the sum total of our experiences into balance and in tune with our current lives.

Any thoughts we have about the future may or may not come into being. We might have aims and goals that are essential for steering the direction of our life, but the present is more real than anything else and is where we can do our most productive work, both on ourselves and in the wondrous and creative world in which we live.

If we expect the future to unfold in a manner that we desire, we will probably be constantly disappointed and miss out on new possibilities unfolding in our lives. If our heads are in the clouds we are likely to lose our way. It is where we are now and what we do with our lives in the present that is important. If we are not happy with anything in our life or unfoldment, we will need to discover why and find ways in which we can constructively deal with any problems we may have. Through this we find our lives taking on more meaning and purpose.

Spiritual unfoldment does not entail escaping from the realities of life, but taking responsibility for our actions and reactions and learning to *be* in the present. Nor does it imply becoming someone else or seeking some kind of mind-blowing experience. It means waking up to the wonder and beauty of life, to our own unique selves (the human brain alone is possibly the most complex mechanism in the universe) and realising there has never been anyone on Earth like us. It is about being right where we are and allowing our mind and heart to open. Nothing could be simpler and at the same time such a sea of trouble. The mind is like a constant thought factory keeping us from knowing ourselves, whilst our emotions invariably carry us to places we feel we ought not to visit. Yet this is all grist for the mill and a part of spiritual unfoldment. For learning how to be aware of these things is a crucial step towards change and positive growth. To live fully is to be open to every minute of our lives – to see life as it is and experience it as if for the first time, unprejudiced by any spontaneous reaction or restrictive view and allowing such experiences to influence our actions in creative ways. There is potential for growth in every moment if we are prepared to awaken to it.

Mindfulness, awareness, attentiveness, contemplation or remembrance are terms used by different traditions for a variety of practices and states of being that help to centre, open and calm our minds and emotions and free them from ordinary judgements. Mindfulness is particularly popular in Buddhism and can be used to bring about awareness of the transient nature of all things. Attentiveness and contemplation are forms of prayer found in the Christian mystical tradition. Remembrance is a Sufi practice. By performing exercises such as these we are able to surrender the small self and be receptive to and interactive with the present in ways that we have never experienced before, as the present is always a new experience, yet most of the time we are not open to it. Life can all too easily pass us by, whereas conscious living helps us notice what is happening externally and internally and become aware of our actions and their effects upon us and others. We sometimes hear people use the expression 'I forgot myself' when they are careless or lose their tempers, which in these instances signify states of unawareness. Not to be confused with the practice of self-forgetting (selflessness) performed in many spiritual traditions.

The art of being mindful or aware is about maintaining an outer and inner observance, noticing how we act and respond to life. The basic aim is to experience the present without any pre-set judgement, to apply ourselves consciously and selflessly to whatever we do and find an at onement in each moment. The practice of mindfulness breathing (breath awareness) is particularly helpful for centring our awareness and can be practised by bringing our attention back to the breath throughout the day. This can be done by mentally noticing the breath passing in and out the tip of the nostrils, or observing the abdomen as it rises and falls.

Attentiveness or contemplation may be used for centring and calming our thoughts and becoming receptive to a greater Divine power that can interact with and influence our life, which helps us to discover a sense of God in everyday activities and in our interactions with life and people. Remembrance requires reciting a short formula in order to 'remember God often', which, like mantra or chant, can bring about a highly clear, energized and open state of perception. Through such practices we are able to recognize the sacred in all and purify our hearts. For it is within the present moment that we can awaken to finer and less self-centred qualities, transform our weaknesses into good, be open to joy, peace, love, contentment and beauty in the world around us and creatively participate in life as it unfolds.

As you read these words, observe where you are now. Are you aware of the book you are holding and the colour and texture of the pages? Are there any sounds that can be heard, such as bird-song or people moving around? Are you aware of your body? Where are your thoughts and feelings? Are you in the present moment or have you drifted someplace else?

Everyday sounds or objects can be used as reminders for checking where you are and bringing your attention back to yourself throughout the day. The Vietnamese Zen Buddhist monk, Thich Nhat Hanh, recommends practising mindfulness at red traffic lights, or pausing before picking up a ringing phone: being fully conscious as we move towards it, lift up the hand-set and speak to whoever is on the other end. There is a sign just below a warning light in my bathroom that says 'FAN Failure'. I have translated this to mean 'Full Awareness Now Failure' and find it extremely beneficial to start the day with a shower whilst being humorously reminded to be fully present. You may wish to find your own methods and use your own creative skills to see what works for you.

5. Investigate and welcome all lines of thought that will inspire and help you to grow and develop.

We should not limit ourselves only to one view, but realise that growth is brought about by acquiring receptivity to new knowledge and experience whereby we look into the mysteries of life and the secrets of nature and begin to live and understand the deeper implications of a spiritual life.

Knowledge that we possess today might be right for where we are now. But we need to guard against holding on to views that may eventually stop us from developing further and seeing life from wider perspectives. The sign of a healthy and mature mind is to be able to accept a variety of opposing views and possibilities. Truth often unfolds and changes us gradually – we would probably not be ready to accept its deepest implications otherwise. If we are open to investigating life and new ideas and discovering what truths can be found within them, our development will unfold naturally and lead us onto higher ground. But we must be careful of chasing knowledge that only stimulates our intellect and realise that truth does not confine itself to concepts. This does not mean there is not a level of truth to be found within them. Life is the finest teacher and can help us to find the greatest wisdom within.

6. Seek the company of those with an open mind and sound knowledge of spiritual unfoldment and let their influence encourage you in your search. If you cannot find such people in the flesh, then search for them in the many books that have been written on development.

In the early stages of unfoldment, the company we keep can affect us. Those who live the spiritual life to the full can inspire us to be more spiritually aware and persistent in our search, whereas others who have limited understanding of such matters can weaken our commitments.

This is why reading spiritually inspiring books is beneficial as it opens our minds to wider possibilities of spiritual growth.

It is only once we have strengthened our spiritual consciousness that we will be less affected by negative company. But it should be noted that our judgements about others may be more of a reflection of our own minds and characters rather than of the people themselves. It is not uncommon for individuals to start out on spiritual paths without knowing anyone to turn to for advice, but as they continue in their search, good people often appear and point them in the right direction. The synchronistic law of attraction comes into play and often draws those of like minds together. There are however people who can mislead others, individuals who may have closed views or wrong motives. This is where we have to rely on our own wisdom and intuition and make independent decisions about our growth, as responsibility for it lies in our own hands.

Discernment is required in order to discover what is right for our needs, nature and unfoldment. This applies not just to people we may encounter, but also to our environments and life in general, as well as any knowledge that we discover. There will be times when things seem to strike a chord. Something inside us often profoundly recognizes and responds to truth when it is found. It may be simply a feeling of wanting to unfold better qualities and to contribute more to life and find ways to help others. A young friend wrote after reading something that triggered this response within him and the following extract demonstrates this clearly: "The writer wrote with conviction that seemed mysteriously to reassure me in a way and refresh my direction. It certainly made me introspect and say, 'Yeah, I could be trying harder, be kinder and more thoughtful'."

7. Develop a compassionate heart for all – a compassion which knows no boundary or prejudice.

Compassion is the highest quality we can awaken within us. True compassion is unconditional and reaches across all boundaries. It is a quality of the heart that is limitless and can have a transforming effect upon all who are touched by it. Yet we cannot force ourselves to manifest compassion; it must arise as a natural response to connect with and feel more for life and others – to wish all peace, love and contentment in their lives and do whatever is within our powers to help others when they are in need. We can however work *towards* uncovering compassion, finding it within and expressing it more purely in our lives. This can be done by opening to an all-embracing awareness of ourselves and others, by practising positive affirmations that help awaken finer qualities and by regularly meditating, practising prayer, contemplation or breath awareness, or by becoming involved in selfless activities that benefit other people and life on Earth. These will help us to quieten our minds, transcend limiting perceptions and open our hearts.

But there are times when compassion can mean saying 'No' in order to help someone stand on his or her own two feet, or to honour our own selves when our needs are not being met. There are no set rules. Every situation is different. If we allow it to happen, a generous nature can be taken advantage of. Only wisdom can guide us in such matters. It is for this reason that some regard wisdom as more important than compassion.

The more open we are to ourselves and others, the more free-flowing compassion will function and the greater our capacity to love and receive love will be. When we can do this, we will naturally reach out and embrace others. If we persist in our search to discover the good that is in us and overcome anything that separates us from external life, other people, the natural world and our true spiritual nature, we will find our hearts opening automatically. We will discover a well of unconditional universal love from which we can draw.

Through awakening our lives to compassion, we heal any barriers that we may have created around our hearts. When the heart is firmly rooted in compassion, there are no boundaries left to limit our capacity to love – kindness and non-harm go out to all. The scientist Albert Einstein made the following wonderful observations about compassion:

A human being is a part of the whole, called by us the 'universe', a part limited in time and space. He experiences himself, his thoughts and feelings as something separate from the rest – a kind of optical delusion of his consciousness. This delusion is a kind of prison for us, restricting us to our personal desires and to affection for a few persons nearest to us. Our task must be to free ourselves from this prison by widening our circle of compassion to embrace all living creatures and the whole of nature in its beauty. Nobody is able to achieve this completely, but the striving for such achievement is in itself a part of liberation and foundation for inner security.[2]

Be still and quiet for a few moments and repeat, 'Compassion is my true nature'. Feel it permeating your whole being and expanding to include others.

8. Be at peace with yourself – your emotions, mind and body – and in harmony with all people and all things.

The process of spiritual unfoldment has a practical side to it. For if we cannot find peace internally we will not discover it externally. Those who are able to let in life and live with understanding and a level outlook are true masters of themselves. Through being centred and at one with ourselves we are not bound by any thoughts, feelings or actions, but even-minded and free to act creatively in any situation. We need to see through any appearances that limit us to any person, place or thing and develop open and intuitive minds that recognize the unity we share with all life on our precious and sacred Earth.

9. Avoid resistance to change. Welcome it as a means for growth and understanding more about life.

All things are subject to change. Life is never static, but continuously moves in new directions and is eternally unfolding and transforming. Whether we like it or not, our bodies are constantly changing with time and life is wondrously evolving. Yet only when it appears that things are not changing should we be concerned, as it may indicate that we are stuck in a groove and in need of moving on. When faced with disappointment because events have changed beyond our control, we need to question whether it is caused by our own mind's desires for circumstances to be different from what they are. Is it because we are trying to impose our own notions about how things should be? Are we perhaps putting up resistance to change and the opportunity to grow?

We may not have control over everything that happens around

us, but we can make worthy use of life by wisely learning from our experiences and so become more spiritually empowered influences in the world.

Inner disturbance and imbalance are often created by the way we react and respond to life. We need to begin our spiritual work by finding out what it is that causes us to react and apply appropriate actions that will restore peace and equanimity. We may hold situations or others responsible for making us unhappy or annoyed, but it is our own minds that ultimately create these negatives within us.

When change happens, we need to ask ourselves, 'How do I feel about it?' and 'Do I see change as good, bad, challenging, exhilarating, draining or frightening?' If we respond negatively, we will need to find out what part of us requires looking after. What area of ourselves is feeling insecure or threatened? Sit quietly for a few moments and ask yourself these questions and reflect upon your responses towards change.

Going through dramatic changes can be hard without some stability and a reliable network of supportive friends or helpers. We might have ourselves to blame for facing changes on our own as we may have become too independent. Sometimes it takes a little humility to pick up the phone or write a letter to inform someone you are in need of some support or comfort. Instead of imposing unrealistic demands on ourselves, it can be extremely liberating to admit that we are only human, with feelings, fears and concerns just like anyone else!

10. Cultivate thoughts that are good, wholesome and creative – ones which will help to bring about positive transformations and do not limit the potential you have.

Negative thoughts and emotions unsettle our minds. Whatever is fed into our unconscious mind will eventually take root and have some form of effect. If we are constantly negative, then negative we will be. If on the other hand we endeavour to be more conscious of how we think, feel and act and cultivate more wholesome qualities such as love, unity and friendliness, we will become more positive, healthy and creative. This will provide us with the strength to be more spiritually whole, caring and compassionate. We will be putting into action the law of cause and effect and find more positive areas opening up in our lives.

I was recently asked by someone who knew me if I had been doing any spiritual work. I wondered what the person meant. Did he want to know if I had done any altruistic work or about any creative or kind acts I may have performed since seeing him last? Or did he want to know how much I had been looking at myself, about any restrictive patterns of thought or negative feelings I may have worked on or higher states of awareness I might have awakened to? When I asked for clarification, it turned out he was enquiring about psychic powers. This is a popular misconception that some have about spiritual work. Our soul's journey calls us to follow individual paths that help us to discover our authentic spirit Self in order to embrace actions and abilities that are unique to our personal spiritual growth. There are no set categories of roles to take on, as individual unfoldment implies discovering what *we are uniquely born to become* and the realisation of how unfulfilled our lives would be if we ignore our true callings and the gifts that can unfold as essential parts of our true being.

For some, these gifts can be of a psychic nature. However, although such abilities as healing and clairvoyance can become a part of our lives, not everyone who is awakening to his or her spiritual Self will display or manifest them in the traditional understanding of these words, as people's paths can lie in different directions.

Gifts such as healing and clairvoyance can have great use and impact on many people's lives and be essential facets of their unfoldment. But they are not the whole of what growth is about, which embraces both our individual and our authentic spiritual nature and becoming a more responsible, kind, understanding, creative and compassionate human/spiritual being.

11. Be thankful for any acts of kindness shown to you and repay them by doing good for others. Let goodness flow from you naturally. Perform good deeds purely for the sake of doing them without seeking praise, recognition or reward.

If anyone has been a good friend or shows us some form of kindness, we must always be thankful and return these gifts whenever they are in need. We also need to expand the good we do by helping others whenever we can.

Some become disillusioned with human nature if people do not show appreciation for the work they have done. But seeking reward for any good we do is the wrong motive. Serving humanity is about giving oneself without personal gain or interest. It does not necessarily imply taking up a public cause, which in some cases can mean performing acts and imposing views on others for the wrong reasons.

The right motive is simply to do good – by thought, word and deed – in all areas of life, even if it goes unnoticed. Sometimes, it is simply a matter of being there for others when they are in need. Yet no action is without consequences as there is joy in giving and good always returns in some form or another. It may not necessarily come from the people we have helped, but from someone or somewhere else. We could simply wake up one morning and find that something has changed for the better. Potentials may unfold that we did not know we had, or we might catch sight of a beautiful flower or hear the sweet song of a bird that opens us to the experience of universal love. This is why receiving and being open to good is as important as doing good. Otherwise we are stopping it from entering our lives and denying others the opportunity to manifest any kindness. If we continuously push good things away, they will eventually do as we command and our lives will be less rich because of this. "Consider the one who allows ninety-nine pieces of praise to pass them by, hearing only the one slight criticism, and taking huge offence", Simon Parke points out in *The Beautiful Life*.[3]

Some people find it difficult to accept even the smallest kind acts or gestures that others display towards them, whether it be in the form of friendship, help or complimentary words. There may be many reasons for this, such as pride, stubbornness or low self-esteem. These will have to be addressed if we wish our lives to be open to the good that we have and is around us.

Being open and receptive to good can be like opening our lives to miracles. Things may happen just at the right moment. A book or a person might come along when we need them, or an experience could open us to a greater understanding of life just when we thought of giving up. But we should not think that because we do charitable deeds or some good has come into our lives that it implies we are any further along the spiritual path than anyone else – spiritual pride can be the downfall of even the most accomplished students of the spiritual life.

Rather, we need to be thankful simply for the opportunity of being allowed to manifest some kindness and for any good we already have or that enters our lives.

12. Be conscious of your thoughts, words and deeds and develop creative and wholesome intentions behind them.

Life on our beautiful Earth is too short to waste. We need to abandon all harmful views, talk and actions, concentrate on how we can develop, change what is unnecessary and live more freely and openly in the present. We can often get drawn into being negative. This is why we need to cultivate a strong and skilful will along with self-awareness. If the will is developed healthily it can help change harmful patterns of thought and behaviour. But it needs an element of flexibility, otherwise there is a danger of becoming too rigid and narrowly focused.

To bring about change can be gradual. But if we make the effort to unfold a pure heart, creative intentions and non-harm in all that we do, we will find ways of living our truth and awakening to our spiritual consciousness.

13. Have the humility to apologize when you are in the wrong and accept others' failings when they appear to make mistakes.

We need to take responsibility for our actions and be mindful that others have feelings too. If we are too proud, we can hurt others without even being aware of it.

Our faults ought to make us aware that none of us are actually perfect – which gives everyone their own uniqueness – and make us more accepting of others' failings. If acceptance seems too difficult, we should try to forgive, whether it is ourselves or others. Acceptance and forgiveness often go hand-in-hand. But we must realise that a superficial forgiveness can still mean holding on to some hurt or injustice that we feel should not have happened. True forgiveness can however be a powerful step towards letting our emotional wounds go. This does not imply that we do not make a stand when peace and justice are being threatened. Just as we take steps to restore peace in our lives, whenever it is within our powers to do so, we need to also take actions to preserve peace and injustice in the world.

Sometimes simply apologizing can heal years of conflict between ourselves and others who may have become our enemies. Everything we do is interconnected. If there is friction in one part of our life, it will affect the quality of peace we have in other areas; just as when we experience love in one area, we encounter better relationships in other areas.

Sit silently for a few minutes. Bring to mind someone who has hurt you and repeat, 'Forgiveness is my true nature'. As you say these words, take a deep breath and let go of any negatives with the out-breath.

14. Learn from any situation that interferes with your unfoldment.

We may feel that we have made great progress in our unfoldment, then something happens that reminds us that we are not as far along the spiritual path as we thought. We need not be cast down if this happens, but realise that such things are sent to try us and help us to be stronger in our unfoldment. Problems often make us question things more deeply, which can lead the way to unfolding greater wisdom and insight. If life were always easy, unfoldment would be a simple matter. If something has gone amiss in our lives, then we will need to try to rectify it. Even if we fail, we should realise it is in the trying that stronger foundations are built and that from mistakes and failures we develop and become more wiser individuals.

There may be times when we feel like running away from or discarding things we do not like. We might try to throw away experiences, emotions, people or situations. If we do this, we will never be able to achieve anything in our unfoldment. In every situation there is the possibility of change and of doing some good. Obstacles can draw our attention to what requires looking at within our lives. They can teach us something about the way we work and help us to understand more about life and how we respond to it.

There may be times when we react badly to events. If we observe what is going on and investigate what this is about, what core issue is behind it, we will discover that we are never angry, unthoughtful or unsympathetic without a reason. Often it is because we are discontent and suffering mentally, emotionally or physically. We may even have become a certain way for so long that we identify our personality with being that way. Due to an unsupportive environment we may also feel unfulfilled because our spiritual potential is not being allowed to surface. This is invariably at the bottom of many issues.

See if you can discover a particular negative quality that troubles you, something you have carried for a while or often trips you up, such as anger or a lack of self-worth. Ask yourself, 'What can I do to overcome it?' 'Are there any qualities of my higher spirit Self that can be used to help me to change it?' 'What need is not being met?' 'What plans can I put into action?' 'Are there any goals that need setting?' Sometimes outer debris will need clearing away before seeing what lies beneath it.

15. Be truthful to yourself and others.

In Shakespeare's *Hamlet* Polonius advises his son Laertes, "This above all, to thine own self be true. And it must follow as the night the day. Thou canst not then be false to any man." Truthfulness encompasses being true to our nature, open to ourselves and others and having no delusions about who we are, what we feel or have experienced. It does not mean that we become negative about ourselves or judge ourselves harshly, but accept both our positives and negatives – which in itself is a positive act – and see things for what they are and recognize the good that is in us and others.

It is by coming to terms with all levels of our personality and realising there is more to life than the different roles we play that our true spiritual nature is found. It is also through all levels of our being that our authentic spirit Self seeks to find harmonious and creative expression. In Indian traditions the symbol of the lotus (a type of water lily) can depict the flowering of enlightenment. The lotus grows out of the mud at the bottom of ponds and flowers on the surface with its petals open to the rays of the sun.

16. Let go of any restrictive thoughts or emotions concerning people, things or situations – anything that stops you from recognizing the sacred in all.

Although life is about growth, we cannot freely and healthily move forward until we let go of where we have been and leave any restrictive patterns behind. If we are loaded down with too much baggage we will not be able to travel far. We need to look for ways to change creatively and move on from any troublesome thoughts or emotions. They are after all, merely distorted qualities of who we are and often cause the appearance of separation from our true spirit Self. Remember the humorous story about the seeker of truth who was asked how he was, to which he replied, 'I'm perfect, but having trouble manifesting it!' Though the idea of perfection in this story is something that is impossible for anyone to live up to.

We may not be consciously aware that we have narrowed our outlook on life, for it could have happened slowly over the years as a result of various negative experiences. We might have become isolated, defensive, cynical or over-reacting because of this, and notice that we sometimes sabotage our creative selves by putting up obstacles that hinder things we do or how we act. Whenever we hear ourselves saying we 'cannot' do something, we need to check whether it is because we have underestimated our potential and abilities, as self-imposed limitations become fulfilling prophecies.

To achieve liberation from unconscious negative forces within us, we first have to become aware of them. Through awareness, self-enquiry and knowledge of who we are and what is happening at deeper levels of our being, we can turn our negatives around and bring about positive changes in our unfoldment. Through knowing ourselves – the good, moderate and shadow parts of ourselves – we come to terms with various levels of our being and find ways of bringing our whole self into balance. This means overcoming our barriers, transforming and letting go of the things we hold onto in order to make room for our higher spiritual Self to manifest and permeate our lives – finding space for that part that can transform and lead us to fuller expression and growth. Instead of being ruled by inhibiting qualities of our nature, we discover power over them and creatively bring about healthy unfoldment.

Realise that everything you experience is a product of your own mind's perceptions. Right at this moment you have all you need for making you happy, fulfilled and contented. How you respond to life is your responsibility. The Zen Master, John Daido Loori, pithily reminds us of the following:

Whenever a threat, barrier, or obstacle pops up, our immediate reaction is to pull back, to prepare mentally or physically to fight or run. If you become the barrier – become the fear, the pain, the anger – by experiencing it fully without judging or avoiding or running away, and then let it go, there is no barrier. Actually, there is no way to pull away from it; you cannot run away. There is nowhere to run to, nothing to run from: it is you.[4]

17. Realise that growth is brought about by knowing who you really are.

"The unexamined life is not worth living" the Greek philosopher Socrates once said. Through self-knowledge we become more aware and mindful and begin to see what actions are required for bringing about a healthy openness to life. For no one can know the contents of our own minds, strengths, weaknesses, pains, passions, joys and pleasures better than we do ourselves. It can take courage to see into our emotional households (our desires, fears, negatives and darkest experiences) and face, accept and disentangle ourselves from them. But we cannot become truly healthy until we can do this.

Through self-knowledge we change ourselves, become at one with all life, discover new levels that are unbound by any restrictive patterns and find a balanced centre from where we can make all decisions and actions without prejudice. Here we find greater freedom and paths for interacting with life in more profound and fruitful ways.

A simple practice that can help us work towards this is to sit quietly for a few minutes and bring to mind someone we highly respect and make a list of all the qualities we admire about him or her. Then think of someone we dislike and write down any thoughts and feelings concerning that person. When we look at the two lists, we should realise that they are our projections and that both sets of qualities are also parts of us. We have the potential to manifest sunshine or thunder just as much as anyone else. Yet it is only by embracing and working with all realms of our personality that we can truly move forward.

Some people find it easier to accept their negative characteristics instead of their inherent positive qualities. But it is important to acknowledge the good within us and explore how it can be used to transform any negatives and bring about positive growth. If you have trouble doing this, try and bring to mind good deeds you have performed as this will show you that you have such qualities within you. The deeds may be very simple acts. People sometimes think spirituality means making grand gestures and trying to change the world to the way they want it to be. In reality it is often about the small and unselfish things we do and their influence on others and the world in which we live.

18. Accept your complete self.

Sometimes we may think we are being strong by not letting our feelings come to the surface. Yet it is often braver to feel any pain, fear, anger or sorrow we have and through this find a different kind of strength that opens and heals us. To push things away or to deny that they exist only creates inner conflict and delusion instead of growth and awareness of life within and around us.

Acceptance is sometimes misunderstood and seen as a negative or passive state. But it is an integral part of the growing process that leads to opening up, facing and taking responsibility for our life, and discovering how we can truly express and authentically be ourselves more freely and creatively in the present. It does not imply being disempowered by others or taking on board every piece of rubbish people may try to impose on us, but meeting life's challenges with wisdom, accepting what is going on, having creative choices in what we do and finding ways to understand and skilfully deal with any problems placed before us.

Until we have faced and accepted things as they are, we will not be able to decide what actions to take for living healthily in the present and achieving an authentic openness. Instead, we will find a discrepancy between how we believe we and life should be, and our understanding of ourselves and others will be influenced by this imbalance.

When we have knowledge of what is happening beneath surface layers of ourselves, we become aware of any binding or restrictive problems. We can then work towards transforming them by embracing and accepting them, which helps disperse any power we may give to them. By letting things in and owning them, we begin the process of inner healing and start working towards letting go of binding and restrictive patterns in our lives.

19. Be open to things as they are.

The way to wholeness and health is not about forcing ourselves to be good, but learning to be gentle on ourselves, to open our hearts, heal our wounds and transform and transcend any ties that bind. In unfoldment there is much that will need to be healed, understood and attended to. It can be disheartening to come across troublesome qualities, but discovering and being conscious of them and understanding how they affect us and came into being is a part of what unfoldment is about.

In the early stages we may find it difficult to be open to life. Yet with the creative use of insight and experience we can learn how to do this and bring about new understanding. Through drawing on awareness, skilful abilities and wisdom we can balance our internal and external lives and harmonise conflicting parts. By combining a healthy degree of discernment with inner strength and humility, we also learn how to explore ourselves without being inhibited by any weaknesses or imperfections. On one level we acknowledge that we are only human, with a body, mind and feelings. On another we realise that we are much more than this, which helps us to not only accept our life with a proactive attitude, but to understand and accept others.

We must realise that although troublesome qualities may currently appear to be a part of us, they do not represent the sum total of our being and are not true reflections of our authentic spiritual nature. For there are many parts, emotions, thoughts and roles we play that constantly change and are only small and minute facets of a much greater spiritual whole.

It is by uncovering new layers, both positive and negative, that we gain knowledge of who we really are, open up new areas and find ways of changing all that appears to block our growth. Yet we must remember that self-exploration is merely a means to an end and not the end in itself. We need to be careful of becoming over focused on and attached to our individual pains, fears, desires and emotions and different roles and temperaments, as it can lead to losing sight of why we are exploring ourselves. The spiritual search involves discovering the hidden creative potential in our positives and negatives, integrating all parts and realising the universal and compassionate spirit Self that has the power to open us to awe inspiring and profound harmony with all life within and around us.

Sit quietly for a few moments and ask yourself who you really are, who you were before you were born. Then ask yourself, 'Who is it that is thinking these thoughts and what qualities are connected with this level of awareness?'

20. Regularly make time to be still and to unfold and harmonise the various levels of your being.

Our days can be spent by being side-tracked with distractions and noise that cause us to lose sight of our authentic spiritual nature. Regular meditation can help us counteract this as well as instill a degree of self-mastery, which strengthens our spiritual will and places our development on firmer ground.

By making time to be still, we start to awaken not only to our higher consciousness, but also to other levels of our being. We may notice all kinds of thoughts, sensations and feelings rising to the surface. Yet because we are beginning to quieten the mind and take in different parts of ourselves, these distractions should start to lose their power. Balance can be maintained by consciously meditating on the breath or on positive qualities such as love, peace, joy and freedom, releasing and disidentifying from any distractions, clearly observing any thoughts, sensations or feelings that surface and seeing them for what they are without becoming involved in them.

Just doing this and by looking deeply into ourselves, we find a more centred place. Yet attachment to it needs to be avoided as well as denying or suppressing any thoughts or feelings that surface, as these can inhibit our development's *natural progression*. However, if a strong feeling manifests, we may need to understand something about it before trying to disidentify from it. Counselling is worth considering in some instances, as it is not always easy facing things on our own.

Only by separating any judgement or reaction from what we experience can we embrace a state of pure unconditioned openness and be in the present moment. It requires trust in the process for this to happen spontaneously and without force. But we need not worry if we require time to arrive at this; for it is better to accept where we are and realise that awakening to different levels of being is generally safer when it is undertaken gradually and gently. We must never be in a hurry to attain states that are currently beyond our reach, or impose any pre-set limiting ideas about what may or may not unfold, as this can put a strain on our unfoldment and block the way to experiencing and opening to what is happening within and around us now. Unfoldment is simply a matter of being where we are, surrendering, awakening and becoming receptive to a greater truth that can change our lives.

Realise that no time mastering yourself or the art of meditation is ever wasted. Constantly find ways to tread lightly upon the Earth. Be who you are. Skilfully live in the present. Take each day as it comes and let your development unfold and evolve naturally. You may, however, have to persist with any practices that you do and guard against jumping from one to another without giving time for a practice to have a result, as the ego craves for new experience, but gets tired of repetition. So do not let the ego rule you. Become aware of it. Transform and transcend it. Embrace the good within and awaken to the true compassionate and wise Self.

Sit quietly for a few moments and ask yourself what qualities you wish to manifest, then affirm their presence within you.

21. Be responsible for your development and check daily that you are moving towards a greater freedom and openness to life.

Each day can bring us closer to manifesting our spiritual nature more purely. Those who are committed to the challenge and constantly work towards a more integrated and holistic life will reap the rewards of finding true peace and productive and creative realms of spiritual evolvement. But our motives ought not to be to gain anything that makes us feel more self-important. Such thoughts arise out of the small self's desire for fulfilment and can never be satisfied. The emphasis needs to be on developing in order to be more balanced, responsible, non-judgemental and caring spiritual beings.

As a new self emerges, so too will new responsibilities, as well as deeper and more subtle issues that will need addressing. This is why it is important to reflect constantly upon changes in our lives and our unfoldment, to be receptive to any openings we have and see what wondrous and creative work can be embraced.

Part of spiritual unfoldment is also about being aware of re-occurring cycles. There can be times when we feel lethargic, creative, energized, agitated or peaceful, or we may heal old wounds and work on past issues or our spiritual will. Important work might be done. However, just as life goes through cycles of change, various issues can re-present themselves and need reassessing and working upon. Unfoldment often means going with these re-occurring patterns and learning something about ourselves and various cycles of life within and around us.

Growth is never a straight road from one place to another. It is perhaps best described as an *organic life process* that requires deep awareness of and insight into the garden of our experience, finding ways to overcome all that prevents us from recognizing our true nature and allowing it to have more influence on our lives. Unfoldment takes us through many landscapes and will involve learning how to disidentify from old psychological patterns and transforming them, and bringing all parts of ourselves together into a complete and synthesised whole. Through this our lives become less complicated and simplicity reigns supreme. We become more effective, freer and open and have a heightened response to all that is sacred and noble within and all around us – including our Earth brothers and sisters of the surrounding natural world.

Through opening to what lies within we discover insight into our lives; with insight comes knowledge of who and what we are; with knowledge comes wisdom; and with wisdom we find ways of being free, joyous and open to life and in tune with all levels of our being. We realise our true place in the universe, embrace the unity we share with *all life* and awaken to the intrinsic sacred presence of our authentic spiritual nature.

Exercises

Exercise 1: Discovering who you really are

You may wish to use the diamond shape below for this exercise or draw a larger version of it.

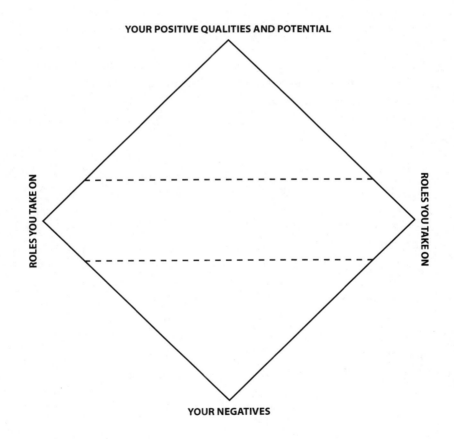

1. Sit silently for a few minutes and bring your attention to the breath. Feel yourself becoming calmer and more peaceful.

2. Ask yourself what qualities you possess and are aware of that reflect your true spirit Self. See what qualities come to mind. When you are ready, write them in the top part of the diamond.

3. Go back to being still and quiet and ask yourself what positive qualities you would like to develop. See what comes to mind. When you are ready, write them in the top part of the diamond.

4. Sit quietly and ask yourself what roles you take on in your life. You may think you are the same person all the time, but there are many sides to your personality. You will discover them in all aspects of your life: your work, home, charitable and social life. Ask yourself what it is you do and identify with. See what roles come to mind and try to give each of them a name, such as the carer, music lover, socialite, loner, critic, healer, crafts person, moaner, worker, activist, housekeeper and so on. Write them in the middle section of the diamond and draw a circle around any major ones with which you strongly identify. Ask yourself what commitments are associated with different roles and how you feel about them.

5. Finally, sit quietly and bring to mind any qualities you do not like about yourself and write them in the lower part of the diamond.

6. You will have now completed a rough sketch of who you are. You may wish to add to it later. Sit quietly and think about what you wrote in the middle section and realise that these are things you do and that you are more than the roles you take on in life. See if there are any positive qualities that are expressed through these activities.

7. Bring your attention to what you wrote in the top part of the diamond and realise that all these qualities are within you now, even those you would like to possess. They are a true reflection of who you really are.

8. Focus on what you wrote in the bottom part of the diamond and realise that being aware of your negatives is the first step to working with and transforming them. See if you can tie up some of the negatives with any roles you take on, or if there is a role you would like to undertake that is causing a negative to emerge because you are not allowing a basic need to be fulfilled or a part of you to be expressed.

9. Finally, see if there are qualities in the top part of the diamond that can help you to work on any of your negatives. At first you might find it hard to see how one part can help another. Just sit quietly and see what impressions, thoughts, feelings or insights arise within you.

Exercise 2: Loving kindness

The following meditation is based on the ancient Buddhist practice of loving kindness, which promotes friendliness towards ourselves and others. Some may find it difficult to practise at first as it can mean facing and overcoming various barriers within themselves. To benefit fully from the meditation, it needs to be practised regularly over a period of time. You may wish to approach the practice in stages, by first working on loving yourself for some weeks before moving on to sending love out to others.

Because the practice is fairly long, you may like to ask a friend to lead you through it or record yourself reading it and meditate to your recording. Be sure to leave an appropriate length of space between each part if you do this.

1. Sit in your regular meditation position and close your eyes. Keep the spine erect as this will allow energy to flow more easily through the body. Become aware of the body and its connections to the Earth. Feel the weight of the body upon the chair or cushion you are sitting on and let go of any tension. Take a deep breath and release any tension as you breathe out. Let your mind become quiet and focus on the breath as you gently breathe in and out.

2. Become aware of any sounds that can be heard and the stillness of the room you are in.

3. Bring your attention to the heart centre (around the middle of the chest), to what is sometimes called the *anahata* chakra. As you breathe in and out, mentally say to yourself, 'I am breathing in' and 'I am breathing out'. Do this for approximately one minute, keeping your attention on the heart centre and on the breath.

4. Silently repeat the words 'I am filled with peace' once for every cycle of breath. Do this for approximately one minute, keeping your attention on the heart centre and the breath.

5. Silently repeat the words 'I am filled with forgiveness' once for every

cycle of breath. Do this for approximately one minute, keeping your attention on the heart centre and the breath.

6. Silently repeat the words 'I am filled with acceptance' once for every cycle of breath. Do this for approximately one minute, keeping your attention on the heart centre and the breath.

7. Silently repeat the words 'I am filled with love' once for every cycle of breath. Let the feeling of love arise within you as you repeat the words. Feel it opening your heart and permeating your whole being. Realise that love is a natural part of you and an intrinsic quality of your true Self. Do this for approximately three to five minutes.

8. Begin to feel love expanding from you and permeating the room. Let go of the phrase 'I am filled with love' and become aware of loving energy in the room. You may wish to bring to mind memories of times when the love within you has manifested. Think of occasions when you experienced love and joy for yourself, life and others.

9. Visualise a close friend sharing in the love you have built. Keep him or her in mind for approximately two to three minutes and mentally say, 'May (name your friend) share in this love'.

10. Visualise a casual acquaintance (such as a neighbour, work colleague or a shop assistant who you know) sharing in the love you have built. Keep him or her in mind for approximately two to three minutes and mentally say, 'May this person share in this love'.

11. Visualise someone you have difficulty with sharing in the love you have built. This need not be someone you know personally, but could be a public figure of some kind. Keep him or her in mind for approximately two to three minutes and mentally say, 'May this person share in this love'.

12. Expand the love you have built to the whole of the building and to the street you are in. Think of some of the houses, the people who live in them and about the plants, trees and wildlife that is also a part of

your street and surrounding area. Let your love reach out and touch all people and life. Mentally say, 'May all that live and grows here share in this love'. Wish everyone and thing peace, love and contentment.

13. Expand your love to encompass other streets and life nearby and to the town you are in. Mentally say, 'May all share in this love'.

14. Expand your love to the whole country and to others close to the one you are in. Mentally say, 'May all share in this love'.

15. Let your love reach out and embrace all countries, oceans, rivers, wildlife and people on Earth and then expand out to the whole universe. Mentally say, 'May all share in this love'. Wish *all* love, peace and contentment.

16. Be still for a while and let love naturally flow from you.

17. Bring your attention back to yourself and take the love you have built with you as you go about your day.

Exercise 3: Body, mind, feelings and spirit

We need to recognize that spiritual growth is about wholeness. In physical life we live in and function through the body as well as through our minds, thoughts, emotions and feelings. These parts of ourselves interact with the greater, larger Self and with the supreme Spirit that permeates all. For any spiritual exercise to have practical foundations we need to interact with every level of what we are. The following exercise is designed to help you be in touch with the many facets of your being.

1. First of all, make sure that you are relaxed and sitting in a comfortable position with the spine erect. This will enable the breath to flow freely in and out of the body and will keep the mind alert.

2. When you feel settled, take your attention to the breath and mentally become aware of it as it passes in and out of your nostrils. Allow your breathing to find its own natural rhythm.

3. Bring your awareness to the body. Feel the weight of the body upon the chair or cushion you are sitting on. Feel the sensation of the hands resting upon your legs or lap. Feel the body sitting there and the sensation of the breath rhythmically flowing in and out.

4. On the in-breath mentally say to yourself, 'I have this body' and on the out-breath, 'but I am more than this body'. Do this for six breaths.

5. Take your awareness to your thoughts. Spend a few moments just being aware of any thoughts that come and go, without becoming involved in them. Simply watch them as a discerning observer. After doing this, mentally say to yourself on the in-breath, 'I am the thinker', and on the out-breath, 'but I am more than my thoughts'. Do this for six breaths.

6. Bring your attention to your feelings and emotions. If you have difficulty with this, think of something that evokes a feeling or strong emotion within you, such as peace, love, agitation, anger, happiness,

laughter and so on. On the in-breath mentally say to yourself, 'I am these feelings/emotions' (whichever it may be) and on the out-breath, 'but I am more than these feelings/emotions'. Do this for six breaths.

7. Now think about the spirit that is a part of you. Think about what this means to you. Be aware of any feelings and emotions that thinking about the spirit evokes within you. Think about how your spirit can guide your awareness, your thoughts, your feelings and emotions and harmonise them into a complete whole. Think about how the spirit within you is a part of an animating creative force of life and needs the body to express itself on Earth.

Now take your awareness to your breathing. As you breathe in, mentally say to yourself with feeling and conviction, 'I am spirit', and as you breathe out, 'Spirit I am'. Do this for six breaths.

8. After you have finished this practice, spend some time in silence and stillness, reflecting upon what each aspect of this exercise means to you. When you have done this, gently bring your awareness back to the room or place you are in and the weight of the body upon the chair or cushion you are sitting on. Come back to your regular state of awareness with a feeling of joy, freedom, appreciation and gratitude for being all that you uniquely are.

The more we know ourselves, the more we transform ourselves
and the more the spirit world flows naturally through
and within us.

Part 2

Twenty-one Steps to
Spiritual Empowerment

Commentary by Glyn Edwards

*S*piritual empowerment entails awareness of who and what we are. It encompasses awareness of our everyday psychological and spiritual selves and finding ways of bringing both into balance with one another. The paths leading to this are not always easy and often require perseverance and drawing upon a variety of creative practices and intuitive skills. Just as we need to practise and have a certain amount of discipline and skill to master swimming, driving a car or playing the piano, we also need to draw upon a variety of beneficial activities and skills in order to discover our true spirit Selves.

But not all stages are about activity and effort. There can be times for rest and healing to take place. If we have recently been through or come to terms with a stressful period in our life, then our emotions may need time to heal. This is why awareness is so important, as it helps us to recognize our needs and see what is required at different points in our unfoldment.

There may be occasions when we feel we have taken a wrong turn. But this is all a part of the growing process. If a musician finds a section of music difficult to play, it would be wise for him or her to focus upon what is wrong and see how he or she can best improve his or her performance. It will require reflecting upon the difficulty, breaking it down into easier to handle segments, working on the problem, improving it and putting it back together again. When this has been done, the previously difficult section will be played with more ease. This tried and tested formula can be applied to almost any difficult task and is a safe approach to any problems encountered on the numerous paths to spiritual empowerment.

We cannot do everything at once and nothing worth achieving ever comes without some effort. Those who try to run before they can walk often end up facing overwhelming difficulties in their unfoldment. So patience and humility are two important qualities worth developing, as they serve us well on spiritual paths. The following steps, commentary and exercises will hopefully help to clarify what various paths of the spirit are about, as well as different levels that affect us and stages that can be encountered.

1. Know that you are an individualised expression of the eternal Spirit and that it permeates all life in the universe.

If we accept there is a part of us that never dies, then we need to integrate this knowledge into our lives, investigate its implications and establish greater awareness of its reality in our unfoldment. As we open up to our eternal Self (the spirit that we are, which is an individual expression of the supreme Spirit) and to the Spirit that permeates all, various changes will begin to take place. We will become more aware of the invisible world of the spirit and its influence and of various responsibilities that are essential for following spiritual paths. We will then find ourselves responding to the Divine and the spirit with more receptivity.

In the beginning it may not be clear that changes are starting to happen. But with patience and openness we begin to see where our previous patterns of thought end and another realm of understanding and activity is starting to unfold and guide us.

Be quiet for a few minutes and reflect upon the spirit within. Recognize that you are not separate from the supreme Spirit but an intricate part of it. You are a spiritual being with infinite positive potential.

2. Realise your mind has the power to bring you closer to the Divine and to finding truth in all things.

Our minds have the power to bring about a deeper understanding of what the Divine is in relation to us and how it functions as us. It is by refining our perceptions and opening our minds that the authentic spirit Self's presence becomes more noticeable and life takes on greater meaning. As we awaken to its influence, we open to our own innate wisdom and gain insight into the reality of the Spirit. We start to see the world and our place in it from a more positive and altruistic perspective and awaken to the true 'I' consciousness within.

This happens because of an increased awareness of our psychic sensitivity. We discover things such as Nature, beauty and everyday activity beginning to have a more profound effect upon us and find all life and experience drawing us to a deeper level of understanding.

Through this we discover the Divine in all as well as the good in all and our view and experience of everyday life shifts to a more harmonious perspective. All life and experience become the substance for growth and reflection and a part of spiritual unfoldment. We gradually awaken and take responsibility for what is happening within and around our lives, and make changes that bring us closer to a spiritual way of life and living.

3. Allow your development to unfold naturally.

We must never force our unfoldment or impose ideas about what psychic or spiritual gifts we wish to develop. Patience and a willingness to be of service to the Divine and the spirit, their influence and implications are all that are needed and are the safest approach to unfoldment.

4. Cooperate with and surrender to the supreme Spirit.

As well as a willingness to trust and cooperate with the spiritual dimensions of life, we need to learn how to let go of and surrender all pre-expectations as we open to various levels of our being in order to experience and be guided by what is unfolding and revealing itself without manipulation. By doing this, we surrender to our own true Selves, our own spirit, to the transformative dimensions of life and the supreme Spirit in all.

This allows space for changes to take place that will bring about positive and healthy growth. Yet this is not always easy. There is a wonderful story about a man who hung on for his life over a cliff. In desperation he cried out, 'Is anybody there?' A mysterious disembodied voice answered from the spirit world saying, 'Just let go and I will make sure no harm comes to you'. He then replied, 'Is anybody *else* there?'

Opening and surrendering to what appears to be unknown can be like this and seem frightening, as it means leaving all regular desires and concepts behind and placing the main direction of our lives in the hands of something we may initially not be certain about. But those who are brave enough to make a commitment to seek the spirit and the sacred and Divine in all will find themselves diving into the depths of direct experience and through this will discover reassurance and confirmation about their life's true meaning and purpose.

5. Cultivate receptivity to the spirit's presence and allow it to influence and guide you in your unfoldment.

Awakening to spiritual potential is not always easy as it is experiential and often about noticing subtle changes taking place. It is therefore important to maintain an awareness of how all things affect us and how we respond to life and everyday experience.

We will notice as time progresses and we open up to our potential, that the call of the spirit – the spirit's influence interacting with our everyday thoughts and actions – will deepen and change. Because of this, it is important not to be inflexible or narrow in our outlook, but open to all possibilities. As we develop a deeper response to and understanding of our sensitivity and spiritual and psychic nature, we allow the spirit's presence to manifest more fully in our lives and guide us onto richer planes of being and consciousness. By remaining open to all possibilities, we find ourselves unfolding a variety of previously hidden potentials and awakening to greater knowledge and insight.

Reflect upon any changes that have happened over the last year. Notice whether your spiritual life has moved on. Have you developed more of an openness to life and others and to wider possibilities and experience? Or is there something holding you back?

6. Awaken to the infinite qualities of good within you.

As we start to open to powers and gifts of the spirit we will find ourselves awakening to spiritual understanding and manifesting qualities such as love, respect, compassion and empathy. These are in fact already inherent within us and are expressions of our true spirit Selves. We may have exhibited them before, but will notice as our unfoldment proceeds, that receptivity to our authentic spiritual nature can have a profound effect, if we allow it, upon the expression of these qualities.

Through manifesting and expressing these qualities more purely, the gift of wisdom increases. Our wise and compassionate natures grow by responding to our true spirit Self's influence. We become more skilfully aware, begin to see life and others from wider perspectives and empathise with others' suffering and struggles more naturally.

7. Develop unconditional love for yourself and others.

To express and manifest unconditional love, acceptance of ourselves and others needs to be cultivated. It is through both love and acceptance that change begins. We start to display love in its purest form: as kind, inclusive, compassionate, understanding, open and unconditional. It is through unfolding love for and acceptance of ourselves and others that we become more centred and peaceful. We express compassion in a fuller sense and embrace, care and feel more for all life. The excellent Yoga teacher and writer Joan Cooper succinctly pointed out the following about acceptance:

> *Acceptance is a conscious act. It requires a considerable degree of awareness, for example, to accept interruptions as events that belong to a particular day; to curb a habitual impatience with someone through accepting the reality of that person's nature, which only he can alter; to say 'yes' to an activity which is usually preformed with reluctance and recognise its place in the structure of the daily life.*[5]

Entwined within the unfoldment of love and compassion is the practice of loving and appreciating ourselves. For if we cannot love and appreciate ourselves we will have no love to share with others. Our well of goodness, compassion and kindness will be empty. The writer and psychologist John Welwood made the following practical observation about opening ourselves to love in his *Journey of the Heart*:

> *Whenever our heart opens to another person, we experience a moment of unconditional love. People commonly imagine that unconditional love is a high or distant ideal, one that is difficult, if not impossible, to realise. Yet though it may be hard to put into every day practice, its nature is quite simple and ordinary: opening and responding to another person's being without reservation.*[6]

8. Embrace the whole of what you are.

We can often be in disharmony with different parts of our being instead of embracing our complete selves. By accepting ourselves, we embrace the whole of who we are: the positive, negative and indifferent, as well as the mind, body, emotions and spirit. This means recognizing and embracing all aspects of ourselves, including parts we may not like or have previously been unaware of. However, we ought not to condemn anything we find, but accept and work with it in order to achieve creative growth and harmony of the whole of our being.

Through self-awareness and self-acceptance we become more observant and conscious of different levels of our being and of various influences that work within and through us and all life. We begin to see, recognize and understand the sacredness of all life from an emotional, mental, intuitive and spiritual point of view. Through awareness of our whole being, we see that our true spirit Self endeavours to influence and guide us, so that we may grow and truly live a spiritual life and express ourselves more freely, openly and healthily.

People become unhappy not because they do not have joy and peace within themselves, but because they do not possess the knowledge of how to unlock them. It is by embracing the whole of what we are that we find the jewel of wisdom that lights and leads the way to treasures of the spirit.

9. Realise that the one creative power in all life is God.

We live in an evolving universe governed by creative power and Divine intelligence. God, which is both masculine and feminine, is the inner essence and cause of all life, the ground of everything and everyone. It is infinite being, bliss and consciousness, transcendent, immanent, omnipotent, omniscient and omnipresent.

This creative power works through us at our individual level of understanding. To open ourselves more purely to it, we have to let go of any perceptions that stop us from recognizing it within ourselves, all life and all people. Through widening our spiritual receptivity, knowledge and consciousness, we awaken to the one in all and the all in one, and to limitless life, power, creativity and potential of our authentic spirit Self. Once we are touched by these things, we must then learn to live by them.

10. Without self-conscious attunement to the all-pervading presence of the Divine, the practices of meditation, prayer and contemplation will be limited.

We need to recognize that the one creative power and law that operates in the universe is God. Unless we consciously make the effort to attune to the Divine in all, we will never understand the spirit that we are and its relationship with everything and everyone. Without this, practices of meditation, prayer and contemplation will be limited.

We live, move and have our being in God. We came from and are a part of God. The very foundations of our lives belong to God. It is the substance, continuity and activity of all life. We derive everything from God. Our mind is God's altar, our body is its temple and our spirit is God's home. All creative potentials and possibilities are within this spirit that we are, which connects us deeply with the creativity of the Divine in all life.

We need to be conscious that it is through our minds, emotions and individuality that we develop the ability to be more Divinity-centred and establish greater awareness of who we are and how we are interconnected with everything and everyone. The more we are able to recognize this reality, the more receptive we will be to infinite qualities of good within us. This will give us the strength to free our mind and emotions and embrace a greater truth to live by. The following exercise is given to help you work towards this goal:

1. Sit in an upright position with the spine erect and become aware of the body. Feel its weight on the chair or cushion on which you are sitting. Be quiet for a few moments then contemplate the importance of the body. Appreciate it for what it is – an essential vehicle for expressing yourself on Earth and living an active physical life.

We often ignore our bodies and do not look after them as well as we should. So give yourself time to listen to and feel into the body and see if there is something it needs. Does it require more love, care or time for healing?

2. Relax the body by quickly moving through it with your mind. Start with the feet and move on to the ankles, calves, knees, thighs, hips, buttocks, lower back, abdomen, chest, shoulders, arms, wrists, hands, neck and head. Use the word 'relax' as you touch each area with your mind and release any tension as you breath out. Pay particular attention to the shoulders, facial muscles and jaw as there is often a build-up of tension in these areas. Gently roll your shoulders and neck and perform a chewing motion with your mouth, then relax.

3. For a short while, become aware of your breath as it flows in and out of the nostrils. Realise that every breath you make feeds the plants and in return their oxygen feeds you.

4. Be aware that you are breathing in a new beginning on the in-breath, and letting all restrictions and limitations go on the out-breath. Do this for approximately three minutes.

5. Feel a sense of peace pervading your whole being and stay with this feeling for a while.

6. On the in- and out-breaths, begin to feel that you are expanding more and more. Feel the energy of this expansion and realise that it is your own spirit's energy. Do this for approximately three minutes.

7. Ask that God's power will make itself known and blend with you in this expanded state. Ask for this power to expand you further. Feel it expanding and blending with you. Do not allow your mind to condition anything to happen. Let any experience arise naturally without force and be at one with it for a while. If your mind wanders, return to the breath and reflect on the Divine and its power blending with you. Do this for approximately ten minutes.

8. When you feel ready, mentally talk to God. Bring to mind any thoughts, hopes, dreams and aspirations that you feel are important. Place them in God's hands and then let go of them with the out-breath. Surrender them to God.

9. Allow the spiritual dimensions of life to manifest within you. Let these dimensions open and guide you to a greater life and awareness of the spirit world's presence. Ask for direction and to be shown what is needed for further growth. Keep the mind relaxed, open and receptive to whatever thoughts, sensations or impressions occur. Do not pre-condition anything. Just sit and blend with the spirit world's presence and power for a while (approximately 15 minutes).

10. Slowly bring your awareness back to the room you are in. Thank God and the spirit world for cooperating with you. Allow this meditation to influence you in your daily life and activities.

This exercise helps you to recognize the Divine and spirit world's power as part of you. It also helps you to understand how to free your mind and become more self-aware. During the exercise you may experience some form of opening that gives your life more meaning, purpose and direction. Your unconscious mind will register this automatically and may bring about various sudden or gradual changes. But do not hold onto any experience or expect it to happen exactly the same again, as this can block receptivity to any future growth and meditation practice, and impede the power and influence of God and the spirit that are around and within you at all times.

11. Accept all negatives as instruments for growth in your life.

Any negatives within us should not be in conflict with our positive qualities and potential. For spiritual growth to happen, we must adopt a healthy attitude towards any negatives we find and ask ourselves what we can learn from them, what brought them about and what needs to be done to transform them. We should view any troublesome thoughts, emotions or actions as friends and teachers on our spiritual journeys. Once we adopt this attitude, acceptance naturally unfolds and possible changes present themselves. As if by magic, the things we found difficult to face and viewed as negative become the instruments for growth and positive transformations. The following exercise can help bring about some of these changes:

1. Become relaxed and aware of the breath. Bring to mind an act of kindness you have performed for someone else. Try to visualise it and feel the kindness you expressed towards that person. Appreciate yourself as a kind and loving person.

2. *Mentally/silently* repeat on the in-breath, 'I (state you name)', out-breath, 'am a loving person'. Do this for five breaths.

3. Mentally repeat on the in-breath, 'I (state your name)', out-breath, 'love you'. Allow these words to take root in your consciousness and accept their true meaning. Do this for five breaths.

4. Mentally repeat with conviction and feeling on the in-breath, 'Love is my real nature'. Out-breath, 'I love who I am'. Do this for five breaths.

5. Mentally repeat on the in-breath, 'Goodness is my real nature'. Out-breath, 'I am a good person'. Do this for five breaths.

6. Mentally repeat on the in-breath, 'Kindness is my real nature'. Out-breath, 'I am kind to myself'. Do this for five breaths.

7. Mentally repeat on the in-breath, 'Acceptance is my real nature'. Out-breath, 'not conflict'. Do this for five breaths.

8. Keep your awareness on the breath as it flows in and out and reflect upon these statements. Realise their full meaning and affirm the truth of them. When you are ready, become aware of where you are sitting and your surroundings and reflect upon any thoughts, impressions or feelings that occurred during the exercise.

12. Accept the creative and positive forces within you and rise above fears, doubts and limitations.

In all areas of spiritual and psychic unfoldment it is important to cultivate and accept the creative side of our nature. This may take time for us to do and will mean observing our minds, actions and reactions.

There are many aspects and levels to our nature, but it is often the appearance of incompatibility between our positives and negatives that causes conflict. Fear especially can be a hindrance. When it comes to spiritual unfoldment, we must never allow fears to hold us back or dictate what we should or should not do. For the life we must strive to live means growing beyond limitations.

Our lives can either be a courageous adventure where we dare to take risks and explore all possibilities, or uneventful and meaningless. Yet before new doors fully open we may feel unsure about the direction our life is taking, which can naturally cause fears to arise. If this occurs, we will have to be aware of it, see where it is coming from and investigate its cause.

Because unfoldment means taking responsibility for our lives and sometimes leads to standing alone for a while, fears may understandably surface. Having the courage to grow and be true to ourselves can indeed be frightening in some cases. Yet we must look upon all experience, including our fears, as teachers and as areas for growth and creatively accept and work with them.

We may also be confronted with doubts about ourselves and our unfoldment. These too need to be faced and questioned in order to see what is behind and can be learned from them. If we are developing spiritual gifts and unsure about certain experiences and abilities unfolding, it would be wise to investigate the source of the uncertainty and see if it is the experience, ability or our response to them that is causing doubts to arise. In this way we begin to look into the experience of doubt and uncertainty. If we keep probing, positive solutions and insights will surface and will provide us with answers and direction.

When we look at people developing mediumistic abilities, we often find them making statements such as, 'I think I saw, felt or heard something'. Instead, we need to contemplate whether or not we are really feeling, seeing or hearing something of a mediumistic nature, and learn how to distinguish the difference between imagination and the spirit working through and with our mind, thoughts and senses. This way developing mediums will begin to look constructively at their abilities. They will then begin to recognize the difference between individual imagination, doubt, receptivity and certainty. It is often just a lack of self-trust that holds people back.

13. Recognize the higher Self and its relationship with the creative principle in all.

Through awareness of our thoughts, feelings, actions and reactions we understand ourselves more fully and see what positive qualities lie within. By acknowledging and cultivating our original goodness, we allow it to affect our unfoldment and bring about changes and conditions that are in tune with its influence. This is all connected to the law of cause and effect. By having a creative approach to unfoldment, we face and overcome our negatives and bring our lives into balance with the higher spirit Self. For our higher consciousness and spirit are parts of the creative force that created and continues to flow through and animate all life. It is only we who limit our abilities, finer qualities and awareness of our life's true nature and purpose.

14. Trust the power of the spirit within.

We must realise that our true spirit Self is whole and without boundaries, and continually seeks to express this wholeness and boundless nature in and through every level of our being and everything that we do. It knows no limitations and has the power to bring about positive changes, congruence in the ways we think, feel and act and enhance all creative abilities and qualities of compassion we have.

To trust the power of the spirit within is to realise that it can only create good and therefore there is nothing to fear and everything to attain by opening to its infinite life affirming possibilities. The more receptive we are to the spirit Self's presence, the more freedom we find in everyday life and the truer we will be to ourselves and others. The universal mind and consciousness of the Divine will function in a less restrictive way within us, through us, as us. We will acknowledge the creative energy of the Divine as an essential part of our own being and how it connects us with all creative life and activity in the universe. Through this we become more purer instruments for the activity of the spirit and less inhibited by the appearance of everyday restraints of life and living.

15. Realise you have within you infinite possibilities and potential.

If awareness is healthily maintained, it will open new doors in our unfoldment. By using it to investigate and increase our spiritual and psychic knowledge, we can grow in wisdom and understanding and awaken our lives to greater possibilities. In the beginning stages the mind may be more familiar with everyday knowledge and thought rather than spiritual perceptions of life. We may feel like "a stranger in a strange land" and be unsure about our abilities, as we often limit ourselves and underrate what we can truly achieve in life and our development.

A way of helping us to overcome any self-imposed limitations is to embrace the power of the spirit within. By recognizing and manifesting this power more purely we find ways to face, rise above and overcome difficulties and obstacles and start to acknowledge, accept and work with the limitless creative potential we have. Affirmations are particularly useful in bringing about these positive changes. By starting with the statement 'I am', we begin to establish awareness of the eternal 'I', which is an intrinsic part of our spiritual being. Statements such as 'I am at one with all the creative power there is' and 'I am infinite potential and express this now' help to affirm the creative and positive parts of ourselves and manifest them more firmly in our lives.

When we affirm our positives, we need at the same time to release our negatives. Statements that help to bring this about are, 'I release all limiting conditions and let go of them', or 'I release all doubt, fear and worry' (release them with the out-breath). By using both types of affirmations, we work on the positive and negative sides of our nature.

We need to realise that every emotion is the result of either positive or negative thinking. It is only through awareness of and creatively working with our thoughts, feelings and emotions that we manifest more positive qualities within our lives. Through being increasingly aware of our actions and reactions, we become more spiritually responsible. Until we have awakened to self-awareness, we can never truly know who we are and fully trust ourselves.

We see that self-awareness is not about limited ideas of spiritual and psychic unfoldment, but the whole of what we are and the whole of an abundant and authentic life. So never allow yourself to be blinded by notions that spiritual unfoldment is higher than everyday experience or physical and intellectual activity, as they are all interrelated and integral parts of one another. Spiritual empowerment is not about blissing out and being uninterested in what is happening around us. Life and how we respond to it are essential facets of healthy spiritual living. Everyday experience is where our unfoldment needs to begin, and intellectual and physical development can be used as beneficial paths to unfoldment.

By being aware of how we act in everyday life, we can grow into more centred and loving individuals, and by cultivating our minds and looking after our bodies, become more active forces for good. All are parts of the process of discovering who we really are and can be used as vehicles for transformation and expressing our true spirit Selves more naturally. With spiritual gifts, the more open and cultivated our mind is, the more receptive we will be to higher and refined influences.

Unfoldment and awareness are about spiritualising and harmonising every level of our being – body, mind, feelings, emotions, psyche and spirit. We cannot have a philosophy for life unless we allow all of human experience to be part of it and develop through this ideas that form the basis for how we live. This needs to be based on fully and wholesomely living our lives the best we can and discovering what is individually suitable for our growth. It means we do not accept things blindly, but discover for ourselves what is right or wrong, just or unjust, and have the courage and conviction to follow our own paths and continually find spiritual truths for ourselves.

16. Treasure and build upon any insights you have and work towards a more integrated and God-centred life.

Any insights we have into life and unfoldment needs to be treasured and built upon. This will help us to draw and rely upon our own wisdom and experience. Through doing this and by cultivating a healthy attitude to life, we find every level of our being becoming more harmoniously balanced. We become much more aware of subtle changes in our psychological selves.

We may think we are the same person all the time, yet there are many levels that can constantly change and affect us numerous times a day. By being aware of these changes we start to understand the process of spiritual transformation and empowerment and how to manifest beneficial qualities of our true Selves.

17. Awaken to the reality that you live, move and have your being in God.

It is through the process of self-realisation that we grow to accept our individual selves as spirit and recognize that this real Self lives, moves and has its being in something even greater – a power that is all-loving, understanding and permeates everything.

We acknowledge that what God is, we are; that our individual selves are expressions of the Divine – that God is expressing itself in and through everything and everyone. By awakening to this reality we discover a myriad of positive qualities within us. Unfoldment then becomes a matter of bringing these to the surface and allowing them to become profound influences that can guide us in our daily lives, which help us actualise the potential of inherent gifts of original goodness, such as creative, mediumistic and compassionate awareness and actions.

18. Reflect upon the authentic Self and become aware of your spiritual consciousness.

In the process of spiritual and psychic unfoldment, we have to find time to look deeply into questions such as 'Who and what am I and where is my life taking me?' and recognize the creative spirit Self within.

Just as alchemists attempted to use their magic to turn base metal into gold, we need to employ every means at our disposal to refine our perceptions. This is why practising affirmations, contemplation and meditation, along with awareness of our body, mind and emotions, makes us successful alchemists, because it is through these that we discover ways of recognizing our authentic spirit Self and bring about life changing transformations. We find methods that help us to refine the base metal of our own being and turn it into gold. The following meditation is particularly helpful for expanding your levels of consciousness:

1. Repeat on the in-breath, 'My body is God's temple', and on the out-breath, feel and know that healing is taking place in the physical body. Do this for five breaths.

2. Repeat on the in-breath, 'My mind is God's altar', and on the out-breath, realise that your mind is open to inspiration and new ideas. Do this for five breaths.

3. Repeat on the in-breath, 'My feelings connect with God's love expressing itself through all', and on the out-breath, be aware of the intuitive level within you opening to expressing itself more freely.

4. Repeat on the in-breath, 'The abilities and potential I possess (whether mediumistic, the ability to love, sing, dance, be kind, to heal and so on) are God's gifts', and on the out-breath, surrender all expectations and needs and leave them in God's hands.

5. Repeat on the in-breath, 'My spirit lives in God's presence', and on the out-breath, realise that nothing limits you. Do this for five breaths.

This meditation encourages you to be more God-centred and to realise that all levels of your being are connected to a creative and Divine source.

19. Let go of anything that creates the appearance of separation from the authentic Divine Self.

Nothing has the power mentally or emotionally to affect us unless we give it our consent to do so. Instead of being bound by the appearance of separation from God and our true spirit Self, we need to find ways of freeing our minds and emotions and embracing a life of truth, harmony, love, joy, peace, openness, unity and compassion. Through this we discover that nothing is worth doing unless it has a spiritual basis for growth and good in our lives and in the world, and how both growth and goodness are intrinsic facets of God interacting with and expressing goodness through us. So let us make our actions at one with our minds and hearts, and our minds and hearts at one with God, so that the spirit that we are may allow its radiance to shine and manifest more purely in our everyday lives.

20. Seek to understand and live life from a higher spiritual viewpoint and harmonise your life with the spirit.

If we truly wish to develop and manifest all that is good within us, we must endeavour to harmonise our lives with the spirit. When we restrict our view and understanding, our world splits into subject and object (seer and seen) reality with no visible relationship binding it together. Like waves rising from an ocean's surface, we see the world made up of individually distinct and separate parts. By deepening our understanding we realise that all is interconnected and are parts of one great ocean of life. Here we find a level of our being in serene balance with itself and all of life around it. It is only the appearance of separation from this reality – created by restrictive thoughts, emotions and perceptions – that stops us recognizing and manifesting it and allowing it to have more influence on our lives and conduct.

21. Do everything as an act of selfless service and for the manifestation of the eternal Spirit.

We have within us infinite qualities of good, love and compassion. Every act, thought and expression can be reflected upon and used to unfold these qualities more purely. By doing this we make our lives a constant meditation and uncover a sense of the inherent universal Self in everyday life. We become less self-centred and more in tune with life and the world of the spirit. For all life is sacred and ultimately derives its existence from God. We therefore need to seek to become one with this sacredness that exists in everything and everyone and respect and care for all life, including ourselves. Anything that separates us from others means separating ourselves from life and the awe inspiring creativity of God and spirit working through all.

Living by spiritual laws means going beyond ordinary laws, taking responsibility for every area of our lives – our thoughts, feelings and actions – and being respectful of everyone and every form of life with which we come into contact. We may not be able to accomplish this overnight, but it is in the trying that we become more caring, loving, centred, responsible and empowered spiritual beings.

Further Exercises

Exercise 1: Creating your own mandala

The following exercise requires using psychic awareness to discover various qualities and potentials within you. It is a useful practice for developing intuition and insight into your true spirit nature.

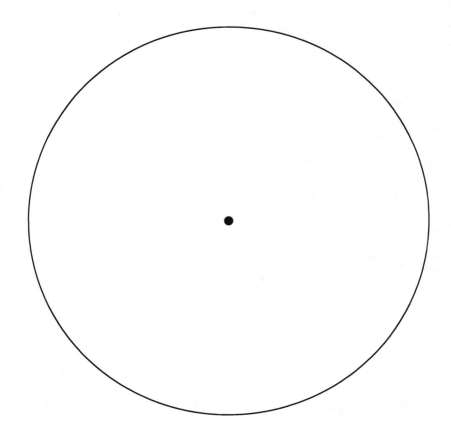

1. Draw a large circle on a sheet of paper. If you do not have a compass, draw around the edge of a large circular dinner plate. In the middle of the circle, draw a small round dot, which will represent the spirit Self. You should end up with something that looks like the drawing on page 75. If you have access to a photocopier, you may wish to enlarge the printed drawing onto a sheet of A3 paper and use that. Within it you will create your own mandala, which will represent where you are now.

2. Sit, be quiet and still for a few minutes and ask yourself, 'Who am I? What is my goal in life? How best can I achieve it?' See what impressions, thoughts or feelings surface. You might find symbols, words, images or colours coming to mind and additional thoughts and impressions rising to the surface as you do this exercise. Whatever impressions you have, draw or write them inside the large circle. You may wish to use different coloured pens and crayons. If you are an artist, you might find it more helpful to express yourself in materials with which you are familiar, such as charcoal, paint or pencil. You could even use stones and objects from Nature and place them inside the circle.

3. Sit quietly again and ask yourself, 'What is my creative and spiritual potential?' Once again, see what impressions, thoughts or feelings occur and put them inside the large circle.

4. Sit quietly again and ask yourself, 'Is there anything holding me back? Is there anything I need or need to do?' Place any impressions, thoughts or feelings inside the large circle.

5. Sit quietly for a few minutes and reflect on what you have created. Look at it, feel into it and see what it tells you about yourself. This will help you to develop the ability to psychically assess your impressions and potential.

Note: In the course of spiritual and psychic unfoldment we might be told many things about various potentials that other people believe we have or do not have. Yet ultimately unfoldment is about discovering what *we feel is right for us*. It involves using our own intuition and psychic awareness and taking responsibility for our own spiritual growth. Though having said this, you may wish to show your mandala to a friend you know and trust and see what impressions he or she picks up from it, as sometimes a different perspective can equally be enlightening.

Exercise 2: Building energy through one-pointed awareness

The following exercise helps to establish one-pointed awareness. It can also help you to become aware of and build your own energies.

1. Sit down in a relaxed position with your eyes closed and rest your left hand on your left leg, with the palm facing upwards.

2. Focus your attention on the palm of the left hand and become aware of any sensations. If the mind wanders, notice this and go back to the palm of the hand. Should any distracting thoughts or images come to mind, do not become involved in them. Keep your attention solely on the palm of the your left hand without imposing any pre-set ideas about what may or may not happen. Even if you experience nothing at all you will have learned something about one-pointed awareness and how to focus the mind.

3. After a while, you may feel energy building in, on and around your hand. Notice this, but keep your attention focused on the palm of the hand. You might begin to sense the energy building and covering the whole of your body. Stay with this experience for 10 to 20 minutes and see what you feel from this energy. A feeling of peace often accompanies it. If you experience this, allow it to permeate your whole being and become one with it.

4. Bring your awareness back to the room you are in and feel the weight of your body on the chair or cushion you are sitting on. Take a slow, gentle and deep breath and experience peace with *all* life.

Exercise 3: Appreciating you

How often have you recognized the good in you and the good you have done? Do you ever acknowledge and accept your good qualities, or tell yourself that you are a kind person? Have you taken time to look at your positive potential and abilities? Have you looked to see if you are aiming towards manifesting the reality of them in your life? If not, why not? What is it that is stopping you from recognizing the good, positive and creative parts of yourself and allowing room for their expression?

You need to learn to appreciate and accept yourself, as well as accept the good that others see in you. Self-appreciation is fundamental to self-awareness and spiritual unfoldment. It does not mean becoming arrogant or egotistical, but simply means honouring the good and the creative abilities and potential that are within you. The following practice is designed to help you do this.

1. Become aware of your breath. Allow your breath to find its natural rhythm. As you gently breathe in and out, bring to mind a good act you have made in your life. As you recall this act, become aware of any good feelings it creates within you. Stay with the feelings for a while, then firmly root them in your consciousness by acknowledging that you are a good, kind, caring and compassionate person.

2. Now look at any good or potential you wish to manifest in your life. Think about the direction your life is taking: the material, mental, emotional and spiritual sides of your life. Ask yourself, 'Am I working towards achieving my full potential and manifesting all that is good within me?' If the answer is 'No', ask yourself why and see what answers arise. Ask yourself, 'What is it that is holding me back?' Look for a way of overcoming any restrictions you may have placed upon yourself.

Once you have done this, visualise yourself achieving your potential and manifesting the good in your life. It might be useful to take a single goal and work positively for a week or more on achieving it. You may find it helpful to keep a journal in which to make notes of any thoughts, feelings or insights that surface concerning this goal, and make a note of anything you may need to do, find out about or change.

3. When you do this exercise try, if you can, to develop a feeling of conviction about achieving the goal you have set. If you have problems doing this, it can be beneficial to use affirmative statements about the unlimited potential and good you have. An example of such a statement could be:

I am a person of limitless good, power and positive qualities. As I say these words, I accept the truth of them and affirm the creative life that is within me. As this life knows no boundaries or limitations, there is nothing I cannot do, manifest or overcome. Goodness and creativity flow in me, through me and from me. I am a part of the creative force that works in and through all life. As this power is an intrinsic part of who I am, I claim a life of continuous and eternal growth. I accept and acknowledge my good and my creative spiritual potential and continually work towards expressing them fully in my life.

4. Finish the exercise by appreciating the outcome and realising how much it will enrich your life to fulfil goals that you have been keeping from yourself.

The manifestation of spiritual qualities
is the demonstration of truth in action.

Part 3

Questions and Answers

$\mathcal{T}$he following questions were discussed by the authors at a meeting in London. A variety of topics were covered that related to the different backgrounds and interests of Glyn and Santoshan and the knowledge and experience they have. One additional question has been added to this revised edition of *Spirit Gems*, which was originally put to Glyn in the book *Realms of Wondrous Gifts*.

Why is sensitivity such a problem?

GLYN EDWARDS: Sensitivity is related to the feeling parts of ourselves and is inherent in us all. All forms of unfoldment, whether spiritual, intuitive, psychic or mediumistic, will have an effect on our inherent sensitivity. As we develop and our sensitivity begins to expand, we may come up against all kinds of obstacles, such as self-doubt, negativity, uncertainty, mood swings and so on. This may also create a sense of mistrust, both of ourselves and others. This happens because our unfoldment and sensitivity are starting to bring about numerous subtle and noticeable changes that relate to various levels of ourselves.

We need to observe this process as it starts bringing about various changes and see how these changes are effecting us. We will need to probe and ask ourselves what we can learn from these changes, as well as accept any feelings that may surface. Caution needs to be taken not to battle with ourselves, but accept ourselves as we are and realise that we are starting to open up more to life in all its dimensions.

Unfoldment is rather like travelling to different countries. We may feel fairly safe staying where we are, but going somewhere new can create all kinds of unforeseen problems. But do we want to remain safe and stay in one place all the time? Of course not! No one really achieves anything in life without being adventurous occasionally.

Through self-exploration we discover changes that need to be brought about starting to make themselves known. This happens through an increased awareness of what is unfolding in our development, both positive and negative.

By accepting our feelings, particularly negative ones, we let them in and own them, without trying to justify or be defensive about them. Unless we increase our level of awareness and embrace our feelings, we will not be able to respond creatively to what needs looking at or understanding within ourselves. Sensitivity is really only a problem if we allow it to get out of hand. This is why some self-discipline and personal responsibility are important in unfoldment. By being practical and using sensitivity in a skilful way, we can manifest all kinds of positive qualities and potential, such as compassion, kindness and understanding. Sensitivity is therefore an important and essential part of all kinds of unfoldment. Being a more feeling person opens gateways to the spirit. It leads to opening the heart, being at one with ourselves, all people and all things and discovering the true spiritual centre of our being.

Do meditation and therapy achieve the same goal?

SANTOSHAN: The answer to this question comes down to the individual and the kind of therapy or meditation he or she is involved in. Neither of them is an exact science. Psychodrama can be one of the most powerful personal development practices to take part in, but will not suit everybody. Meditation too can be about life as a meditation, creativity as meditation and so on. It should not be restricted to the idea of merely sitting quietly, but expanded to being creatively and compassionately active in the world.

On the whole therapy is about building a stronger sense of self-worth and respect and being more openly expressive. Meditation can share these goals. However, there are many pitfalls. Being individually strong and open about our feelings may not necessarily make us aware of others' needs and feelings or the consequences of our actions. We obviously have to guard against this happening.

Therapists occasionally advocate giving voice to our anger, even though it may do little to dispel it, and sometimes seem to go no further than this, instead of owning and working with it. It can feel good to get in touch with and express our anger at times rather than bottle it up, but it doesn't usually achieve anything constructive. Eventually we will have to go beyond merely letting our anger have expression and start taking responsibility for and find ways and means to transform it, or change a situation that is causing it.

Therapy is often about personal goal-setting and invariably seems to be focused on feeling secure before aiming for self-realisation – a realisation of our true spirit Self and its relationship with everything and everyone – which is not always possible. It can imply that those who are unemployed for instance, or financially living from hand-to-mouth, cannot have a spiritual life until their basic needs are met. For some there may be little hope of them doing anything about their situation. Yet having a spiritual perspective in times of trouble is often what pulls people through and helps them rise above their circumstances and find meaning and purpose to their lives.

Ideas advocated by some psychologists could be seen as spirituality for the middle classes, i.e. that we cannot have a spiritual life without money in the bank, a roof over our head and feeling secure. This isn't to say that there is not some worth in such theories. If our roof is leaking or our children are in need of food, it is more practical to prioritise and attend to these before anything else. My point is that not everyone will be able to do something about their circumstances. A spiritual outlook may be all we have left and be the only thing that keeps us going until better circumstances present themselves where goals could be set.

On the other hand, mindfulness meditation practices focus on opening to ourselves without any judgement or involvement in what we encounter, such as impressions, thoughts or feelings. This can sometimes be difficult or overwhelming if we are not spiritually strong and is where therapy can help. It is not always easy to observe in a disinterested way whatever thoughts, feelings or sensations surface. Yet many meditators find they can come to terms with different parts of themselves without undergoing Western forms of therapy, which often looks and delves into everything to see where this or that feeling or thought is coming from. Instead, the meditator is able to understand, accept, transform and transcend any restrictive thoughts or emotions without some of the complex work of Western therapy. However, this does not mean that both methods cannot be combined and of use to one another.

My view is that some meditation practices can be precarious if the practitioner does not have a strong sense of self-worth. The first part of the Buddhist practice of loving kindness (loving oneself) can be helpful in addressing this problem. It is important to be fairly stable and balanced before aiming for wider levels of awareness. This of course can be tricky as we may start out feeling that we are psychologically fine, only to discover that this was merely an outer shell we built to cover various insecurities.

In the West we seem to live complex lives, have become much more isolated than some communities in the East and do not have strong social bonds to support us. These can be problematic if we are starting to unfold and come to terms with various negative parts of our life. Because of this, people in the West invariably seem to carry around more psychological baggage. Therefore, it is safer to look at some of our issues before we try to see through them or try to disidentify ourselves from them. Therapy can be a good way of doing this. Having someone there for us while we examine various parts of or experiences in our lives is extremely beneficial. The way forward may well lie in people joining forces from both traditions and sharing their knowledge and experiences, which seems to be happening in some circles. By doing so, individuals will attain a balance of both types of work.

Therapy at its best should be a two-way learning process where both parties (therapist and client) enter into a trusting and non-judgemental relationship with no preconceived ideas or set formulas.

Coming back to the point about whether the goal is the same, it should be mentioned that it may change as we progress. Unfoldment is not a linear process. We might even come back to where we started and look at old issues again. Only the individual can truly say what his or her goal encompasses, which will depend on where he or she is at in a particular moment of time.

For me, the path, which includes living a more balanced and compassionate life and being responsible for our actions is more important than any *personalised goal*, particularly, as mentioned, goals can change. On the other hand, the realisation of our true spirit Self and allowing it to influence our lives and conduct is a more self-less goal that never changes for the majority of spiritual travellers. Therapy and meditation may at times share the same path. At others they might not. One thing for sure is that both can be used for opening us to different levels of our being and attaining a greater freedom and awareness of and responsibility for life within and around us.

How do we know we are developing in the way that the spirit wants us to?

GLYN EDWARDS: We cannot always be certain that we will know. In my experience I have noticed that development often moves forward in phases. Each one bringing a new expression, experience and activity. This is why it is important not to have definite ideas or opinions about how our unfoldment should proceed or what the final outcome will be. We may have general aims, but we must be flexible enough to be able to change our main focus if wider possibilities start presenting themselves to us.

I do not think we should have set views about the end product as we are continually growing and having new experiences that can affect the direction of our lives. This is why we need to keep sitting, meditating and reflecting upon our unfoldment and allow ourselves to blend with the power of the spirit within and the Divinity of all life. By doing so, any possible potential will be allowed to surface, be cultivated and allowed to express itself in and through us and lead us on to richer fields of being and consciousness.

How do we transcend the ego?

SANTOSHAN: Personally I prefer to think in terms of *including* and *transcending*. Ego is also a bit of a problem word as there are many interpretations. It is not merely about being egocentric, such as believing that our needs are more important than anyone else's. It also refers to a false sense of self or 'I' that we mistakenly believe we are. From childhood we will have been conditioned to think of ourselves in a certain way: as this or that type of person with a particular temperament. Yet people do not cease to be individuals when they transform and transcend this level of themselves. Nonetheless, there is a subjective change in their outlook and understanding of their personality and their relationship to everything and everyone. In Eastern traditions the ego is generally about holding on to a limited sense of self that separates people from their authentic nature.

Western psychology sees it differently and often views it as the main driving force, which can surface in either an inflated or a deflated way, with self-interested aims. This does not stand up to close scrutiny. Zoologists tell us that even some animals display compassion to one another, even when there is no apparent self-interest to be found. I believe our true nature is good. Deep within us is an inherent part that is caring, compassionate and deeply sensitive to others' struggles and suffering. It is through opening to this part of ourselves that we awaken to the spiritual centre of our being and surrender to what Assagioli (the founder of Psychosynthesis psychology) called the 'harmonising will'. By surrendering to it, we transcend limiting perceptions and awaken to a more integrated way of life and living. Even the search for lasting happiness is essentially unselfish, as it can only be truly found by going beyond self-interests, embracing all as a spiritual whole and living a more balanced life that naturally seeks connections with and manifests kindness to others.

We all rely on other people to survive and live healthily. The food we eat and the clothes we wear are generally the products of other individuals as well as Mother Earth herself. We cannot live properly without intimate relationships. We may only extend this intimacy to a few closest to us, but a truly healthy and full life finds deep and meaningful relationships in all areas.

Christian and Sufi mystics write about a spiritual death, such as the 'dark-night of the soul' and 'passing away'. There is a similar notion in Zen Buddhism. Here the mystic undergoes a purification process that makes room for a wider state of selflessness and awareness. It does not imply a total loss of individuality, but overcoming strong attachments to our individual self, attaining a greater knowledge of who we really are, how we relate to life and being able to live this understanding without restrictive patterns of thought or behaviour inhibiting us and causing us to act less than we should, i.e. uncaringly, unthoughtfully, without compassion and so on. Therefore, transcending the ego does not mean excluding it, but changing our understanding of it and overcoming exclusively identifying with it. To see it as only a part of a greater whole instead of central to it.

In order to attain this level of understanding a certain amount of spiritual mastery and discipline are required. Discipline is partly a function of the individual will and also encompasses patience but should not be confused with suppression or force. Nonetheless, it means exhibiting a certain amount of power and creative mastery over our selfish desires and bringing about changes in the ways we think, feel and act. It may sound like a restriction on our freedom, but it actually gives us more flexibility and choice in life.

Instead of being ruled by restrictive patterns of thought and by any emotional dramas that come our way, we are able to take creative responsibility of how we interact with life. Mindfulness and awareness are important, but without some skilful mastery over ourselves we will find that we keep falling back into old patterns of thought and behaviour. This, I believe, is *one way* to start transcending and transforming self-centred limitations and bring about changes in our perceptions. But there are many sides to this (as there are many facets to our personality) and a variety of practices and abilities can and need to be used to help us progress along the path to a less ego-centred self.

What is the most important aspect in development? It seems that many books tell us different things.

GLYN EDWARDS: There are indeed many books with different points of view. Whatever we read or may be told, we will need to start reflecting on what is important for ourselves, come to our own conclusions and have our own insights about unfoldment.

There are many things that can help us reach varying degrees of awakening, such as cultivating an open mind, working with any openings or insights on a regular basis and allowing them to lead us on to discovering a deeper level of ourselves. By sitting regularly and being still, we learn how to enter a state of inner silence that leads to knowledge of our authentic spirit Self and its implications. Through embracing this intrinsic part of ourselves, we awaken to something that can transform our whole being and give our lives more meaning, purpose and direction.

Yet ultimately I would say the most important thing is how our unfoldment affects us – how we allow it to affect us at every level of our being and in every area of our lives. It means developing a growing awareness of our inner spirit Self and its relationship with everyone and everything, and finding ways and means to manifest responsibly and creatively the reality of its existence in the world and our daily lives.

SANTOSHAN: I agree. The important thing is how we live our lives. People often complicate matters by placing *too much* importance on beliefs or on experiences that are encountered on spiritual paths. Important as these can be, if they are *too rigidly* interpreted they can restrict our growth and separate us from life and others.

By focusing on spiritual growth, which involves including other people and species, individual, social and global responsibility and caring about the natural world – of which we are a part – life becomes less self-focused and limited, more of a meaningful and an enjoyable activity and an ever-evolving active process of understanding and interacting creatively with all.

On the one hand some people might think being in touch with spirit personalities as a bit strange. On the other hand these same people might consider being in touch with Divinity as more of a natural experience. What are your thoughts about this?

GLYN EDWARDS: We cannot separate the spirit world from the Divine as everything is interrelated. If, as I believe, all life survives and is interconnected, then why should it appear strange to commune and be in contact with different realms of existence? In all the great wisdom traditions this contact with other realms has been mentioned and has at various times throughout history to the present day been practised. In some traditions people who walked this Earth have come to be revered as saints, gods or goddesses and there are accounts of communication with these people in nonphysical after death states.

We also need to consider how throughout the ages ancestor worship has been intrinsically bound-up with many traditions (even to this day), how there are accounts about those that have been described as angelic beings communicating with various people, and how some have prayed to different individuals, such as saints, as they are seen as intercessors before God who will act on people's behalf. There are also shamans and oracles who are consulted in various traditions and many renowned mystics have displayed mediumistic types of abilities.

It seems to me that there has always existed in humankind's psyche the belief in nonphysical realms of existence. Early indigenous people and shamans were the first to connect with a spirit world permeating

Nature and to communicate with their departed ancestors. Others have looked towards the more transcendent areas of spirituality. Although there are some who have never completely separated themselves from some of the early indigenous beliefs and practices, there are some who have, which has led to an unhealthy separation between Nature and the spirit. All areas need to be included in the search for the one ultimate reality that expresses itself in and through all.

If we accept that life is eternal and there are other realms of existence intertwined with our physical world, then it must surely be a natural step in our evolution to be able to commune with these other realms and with those who are eternally living on. We need to recognize that there are different ways in which to approach the many-faceted dimensions of spirituality and be open to numerous areas that can lead us to healthier states of spiritual being and embrace the all-ness of what eternal life is about.

All that matters is
what we do in the present moment.

Part 4

Guidance and Inspiration from Contemporary and Past Teachers

*T*he following quotations are from various traditions, disciplines, teachers and writers and use the spelling and punctuation of the books in which they were published. What is written needs little introduction as the teachings and descriptions of various levels of experience speak clearly for themselves. We have attempted to find passages that tie in with the rest of this book, with a leaning towards the practical and explanative in most instances and the inspirational in others. For subjects linked with everyday awareness we have drawn mainly upon contemporary writers who obviously have more knowledge of the problems of modern day living.

We sometimes hear people say that teachings from different traditions should not be mixed and that we ought to keep practices 'pure'. But anyone who studies the growth of any tradition soon discovers there is little that can be placed under such a heading. All teachings evolve out of what has gone before – even though they may have new wisdom and perspectives to add – and are developing and changing all the time. Yet in all of this there are some aspects that are fairly universal and all-embracing and it is these that we have tried to include, although descriptions around ideas of ultimate reality rely on using words that are often inadequate and many have their own interpretations. But these days the focus is generally clear. It not so much where we are going or speculating on metaphysical notions that are of prime importance – as there must surely be levels beyond our understanding – but where we are now, how we respond to life, the Earth, Nature and others and manifest the reality of our truths in everyday experience.

Many individuals are seeking healthy dialogues with people from different backgrounds, cultures and disciplines in order to learn from one another, as well as from past mistakes and misconceptions. Most are seeking ways to move on, improve and adapt their understanding and to find teachings that fit the needs of practical living in the world today and current spiritual issues that we collectively face as a human race. The following pages are for those who wish to overcome boundaries, develop further, have their own insights and understand more about spiritual life from various perspectives and stages people have encountered. May the wisdom of all ages spur you on in your unfoldment and help you to interact more creatively, compassionately and deeply with life.

On being human

In ordinary consciousness, our conditioned self-interest limits us to seeing and paying attention only to that one percent of difference – to the almost total exclusion of our common humanity. Occasionally we do catch a glimpse of how much we have in common, as when we behold great beauty, or when we are united by a powerful desire for peace or justice. But such moments come rarely, and are swallowed up all too quickly by a flood of conditioned thinking that once again rivets our attention on how this person insulted us or that country offended us, how life would be perfect if only we had just a bit more money or opinions were shared by those in power.

– EKNATH EASWARAN.[7]

Humanity as a whole requires us to love and care for all. That is the condition for becoming a true human being. All the great ideals, positive attitudes, and creative forces grow in the heart after becoming a true human being, and we naturally move on the path of transformation.

– SWAMI RAMA.[8]

Beginning the search and finding traces

[S]piritual development is … an adventure through strange lands full of surprises, difficulties and even dangers. It involves a drastic transmutation of the 'normal' elements of the personality, an awakening of potentialities hitherto dormant, a raising of consciousness to new realms, and a functioning along a new inner dimension.

– ROBERTO ASSAGIOLI.[9]

So the man looking for traces finally stumbles upon them – not in the sublime scriptures where he thought they were, far above everything that bothers him. The traces are right in the middle of daily life, amid our daily chores, troubles and hang-ups, and they are conspicuous … wherever I look, there are traces everywhere. That produces the first serious upset in the practice.

'What have I let myself in for? I am getting worse instead of better! This is not leading out of suffering.' For it is not that I am getting worse, it is only that I am beginning to see what actually is there, and always has been there. Little by little the defence screens behind which I habitually hide myself are beginning to give way and dissolve; and with that a first awareness arises of what a formidable task is ahead.

– MYOKYO NI (IRMGARD SCHLOEGL).[10]

Knowing ourselves

Most people confuse 'self-knowledge' with knowledge of their conscious ego-personalities. Anyone who has any ego-consciousness at all takes it for granted that he knows himself. But the ego knows only its own contents, not the unconscious and its contents.

– CG JUNG.[11]

A soul that desires to attain knowledge of spiritual things must first know itself, for it cannot acquire knowledge of a higher kind until it first knows itself.

– HILTON.[12]

Working with awareness and anger

Mind is the forerunner of all actions.
All deeds are led by mind, created by mind.
If one speaks or acts with a corrupt mind, suffering follows,
As the wheel follows the hoof of an ox pulling a cart.

Mind is the forerunner of all actions.
All deeds are led by mind, created by mind.
If one speaks or acts with a serene mind, happiness follows,
As surely as one's shadow.

'He abused me, mistreated me, defeated me, robbed me.'
Harbouring such thoughts keeps hatred alive.

'He abused me, mistreated me, defeated me, robbed me.'
Releasing such thoughts banishes hatred for all time.

– THE DHAMMAPADA.[13]

Growth in true selfhood does not whittle away my capacity to feel angry or aggressive. Neither does it lessen my need to respond in some way to that feeling. Growth helps me to accept my aggressiveness as a human feeling that is undeniably there. The unfolding spirit of man, moreover, offers each person a wider view of life. It is from this perspective that I may see in a new light the persons, events, or things that arouse my anger and aggression. From this wider view, my anger either subsides, lessens, or finds the right expression in the angry situation. This wider vision itself is born not in anger but in gentleness.

It is not enough to enjoy this wider vision of life; I must also know my anger and its source so that it can be illuminated and tempered by this philosophical or religious vision. A first condition for this sublimation of anger is knowing fully that I feel this way. Next I need to find out why I am feeling so. Only then can I do something about the way I feel in the light of my gentle vision of self and humanity.

– ADRIAN VAN KAAM.[14]

As our daily practice expands, awareness opens to encompass more of our activities. As this general mindfulness becomes established, we notice, for instance, that if all of a sudden anger comes up, we are immediately aware of it. It is acknowledged before it is expressed in words or deeds or becomes out of control. We notice ourselves automatically investigating strong interruptions in the flow. We discover that the sooner we are aware of what's going on, the more space we have in which to relate. When we see ourselves about to get lost in a thought or emotion or desire, we have a moment of choice available ...

This over-all mindfulness is a general scanning that occurs from having encouraged deeper looking. Painful attitudes and desires have less chance to just appear full-grown in the mind when we can see them coming. It's not what arises in the mind that matters, as much as how soon we are aware – mindful of its presence, how soon the forgetfulness of identification falls away. Even a second can be the difference between being lost in a state of mind and the joy which a moment later says, 'There comes that one; how interesting, I'm not pulled by it so much any more.' It becomes fascinating because the realization 'Wow, I'm free of anger,' is often followed by the recognition that we are free from everything at that moment except the pride about how free we are.

– STEPHEN LEVINE.[15]

The art of being and becoming

Be soft in your practice. Think of the method as a fine silvery stream, not a raging waterfall. Follow the stream, have faith in its course. It will go its own way, meandering here, trickling there. It will find the grooves, the cracks, the crevices. Just follow it. Never let it out of your sight. It will take you.

− SHENG-YEN.[16]

Set thy heart upon thy work, but never on its reward. Work not for a reward; but never cease to do thy work.

−THE BHAGAVAD GITA.[17]

Cultivate a generous, open heart. Develop the habit of finding joy in giving, giving. It doesn't matter what you give. Find ways to make others happy. Do not give thought to whether you will receive anything in return … The freely you give, the greater your satisfaction will be. It is more blessed to give than to receive.

− SRI DAYA MATA.[18]

When with others, we should be mindful not to harm them by careless remarks …
    When alone we should examine our thoughts.

− GESHE RABTEN AND GESHA DHARGYEY.[19]

Be happy in the moment, that's enough. Each moment is all we need, not more. Be happy now and if you show through your actions that you love others, including those who are poorer than you, you'll give them happiness too. It doesn't take much − it can be just a smile. The world would be a much better place if everyone smiled. So smile, be cheerful, be joyous …

− MOTHER TERESA.[20]

    [A]nd what does the Lord require of you
  but to do justice, and to love kindness,
    and to walk humbly with your God.

− MICAH.[21]

The universe is sacred.
You cannot improve it.
If you try to change it, you will ruin it.
If you try to hold it, you will lose it ...

See simplicity in the complicated.
Achieve greatness in little things.

– LAO TSU.[22]

To live the spiritual life is to allow the eternal to manifest in the moment without distorting it with the illusions of what we think it is. We can serve this manifestation and fulfil its purpose as human beings. We can turn towards that One Source of all life and open ourselves in love, so that life can flow freely through us and in the world. This turning and opening in love is the meaning of prayer, as we relax into the One Being and allow the Love of God, or the will of God, to flow where it is needed.

– RESHAD FEILD.[23]

The more we try to interpret an experience and clothe it in words, the more we remove ourselves from it. We are left with 'fixed' concepts, and dualistic views concerning the world, so that our responses and reactions to daily situations do not flow from a natural state ...

... we believe that our thoughts and feelings are 'mine'; we judge them in relation to 'my' situation, 'my' life. But thoughts and feelings are not 'me' at all. One thought simply is associated with another thought, and then another ... Each thought involves various words and images, like motion picture frames which are moving continuously, forward or backward, so that the imagery occupies our awareness ...

As we observe our minds, we see that our consciousness easily becomes fixed on thoughts or sensory input. For example, when we suddenly hear a door slam or traffic screech, our minds immediately project an image or concept; and associated with this idea or image is an experience with very precise and exact feeling tones. By staying within the immediate moment, it is possible to enter 'within' the experience. At that moment we discover a certain type of inner atmosphere or environment that has no shape, no form, no specific characteristic or structure ... Therefore to become free from dualistic patterns of mind it is important to go 'beyond' relative understandings and belief, to look inside, and, as much as possible, to stay within the very first moment of experience.

        – TARTHANG TULKU.[24]

Love and forgiveness

Love your neighbour as you love yourself.

        – JESUS (THE GOSPEL OF MATTHEW).[25]

God is love, and those who abide in love abide in God, and God abides in them.

        – THE FIRST LETTER OF JOHN.[26]

Love the wicked man. Why? Because he will then love you, and love will unite his soul with yours.

        – RABBI RAFAEL OF BERSHAD.[27]

Compassion is simply expressing in action the interrelatedness of all life, all being; the person who talks about cosmic unity but does not express it in compassion has not begun to understand it.

        – ROBERT ELLWOOD.[28]

Compassion and love are not mere luxuries. As the source both of inner and external peace, they are fundamental to the continued survival of our species. On the one hand, they constitute non-violence in action. On the other they are the source of all spiritual qualities: of forgiveness, tolerance and all the virtues. Moreover they are the very thing that gives meaning to our activities and makes them constructive. There is nothing amazing about being highly educated; there is nothing amazing about being rich. Only if the individual has a warm heart do these attributes become worthwhile.

    So to those who say that the Dalai Lama is being unrealistic in advocating this ideal of unconditional love, I urge them to experiment with it nonetheless. They will discover that when we reach beyond the confines of narrow self-interest, our hearts become filled with strength. Peace and joy become our constant companion. It breaks down barriers of every kind and in the end destroys the notion of my interest as separate from others' interest. But most importantly, insofar as ethics is concerned, where love of one's neighbour, affection, kindness and compassion live, we find that ethical conduct is automatic. Ethically wholesome actions arise naturally in the context of compassion.

– THE DALAI LAMA.[29]

Compassion is one of the attributes of the spirit. I've said it is so many times. Love, affection, friendship, compassion, mercy, tolerance, kindness, service, are the attributes of the spirit. When you express them you are manifesting yourself spiritually.

– SILVER BIRCH.[30]

In order to develop love – universal love, cosmic love, whatever you would like to call it – one must accept the whole situation of life as it is, both the light and the dark, the good and the bad. One must open oneself to life, communicate with it.

– CHOGYAM TRUNGPA.[31]

Failing to grasp the importance of forgiveness is always part of any failing relationship and a factor in our anxieties, depressions, and illnesses – in all our troubles. Our failure to know joy is a direct reflection of our inability to forgive.

… Analysis and intellectual efforts can produce some softening of the rigidity of nonforgiveness. But true or complete forgiveness lies on a different plane.

Nonforgiveness is rooted in our habit of thinking self-centred thoughts. When we believe in such thoughts, they are like a drop of poison in our glass of water. The first, formidable task is to label and observe these thoughts until the poison can evaporate. Then the major work can be done: the active experiencing as a bodily physical sensation of the anger's residue in the body, without any clinging to self-centred thoughts. The transformation to forgiveness, which is closely related to compassion, can take place because the dualistic world of the small mind and its thoughts has been deserted for the nondual, nonpersonal experiencing that alone can lead us out of our hell of nonforgiveness.

– CHARLOTTE JOKO BECK.[32]

Patience

> In the forge of continence,
> Let patience be the goldsmith,
> On the anvil of understanding
> Let him strike with the hammer of knowledge.
>
> — SIKH MORNING PRAYER.[33]

If one doesn't have patience in daily living one often becomes uneasy and worried. One tries to do things which are not even effective in order to speed up the results of one's plans.

Impatience shows up the ego because we want things to happen the way we have planned them. We also want them to happen at the time we've decided for them. Our own ideas are the only ones taken into consideration. We forget there are other factors and other people involved. We also forget we are only one of … [approximately seven] billion people on this planet, that this planet is one speck in this galaxy, and that there are innumerable galaxies. We conveniently forget such matters. We want things our own way now. When it doesn't happen according to our own preconceived notion, an impatient person usually becomes angry. It's a vicious circle of impatience and anger.

Patience has a quality of insight. One realizes that plans can be made but that anything can interfere with them.

— AYYA KHEMA.[34]

Being a giant in all situations

> Where there is anger, apply loving kindness.
> Where there is evil, offer good.
> Where there is stinginess, be generous.
> Where there are lies, be truthful.
>
> One should not neglect one's own moral good
> For the sake of another's.
> Learn first before teaching another's.
> Let each one embrace his own truth
> And devote himself to its fulfilment.

103

Pay no attention to harsh words uttered by others.
Do not be concerned with what others have done or have not done.
Observe your own actions and inactions.

– THE DHAMMAPADA.[35]

A person's true wealth is the good he does in this world.

– THE PROPHET MUHAMMAD.[36]

The man who does not permit his spirit to be beaten down and upset by dryness and helplessness, but who lets God lead him peacefully through the wilderness, and desires no other support or guidance than that of pure faith and trust in God alone, will be brought to deep and peaceful union with Him.

– THOMAS MERTON.[37]

My son, keep sound wisdom and discretion;
      let them not escape from your sight,
and they will be life for your soul …

– PROVERBS.[38]

Learn to be contented under all circumstances. One who has contentment in his heart finds good everywhere and at all times.

– SRIMAD BHAGAVATAM.[39]

Cherish no hate for thy brother who offends, because you have not offended him … A man's transgressions depend not entirely upon his free choice, but often upon many other circumstances.

– A HASIDIC RABBI.[40]

Practising peace and stillness

All wise people realize that the deeper part of our nature can only be expressed effectively when our outer being is still.

– SWAMI PARAMANANDA.[41]

Be still. Do not think of plans for bringing peace into your life … Dwell now only on His Presence. And be still in feeling. Do not give your feelings of fear and worry additional force by attending to them. Be still also in desire; that is, be single-hearted, desirous only of learning this peace.

'I Am Peace within thee'; within thee, a metaphor to express the nearness, the all-pervadingness of the Spirit of Peace.

Thus we take these words as the Voice of the indwelling Spirit, speaking Peace through our whole consciousness.

With the stilling of thought and emotion will come an illumination, as it were, of our whole being: 'The entrance of Thy words giveth Light', and so from the entrance of this Word of Peace there comes the Light of Knowledge.

From this Peace we draw wisdom and strength for all our needs. For this Divine Peace is vital, life-giving; there is nothing of inertia in it. Peace is not the mere absence of anxiety and fear; it is the state that comes from knowing we are not alone, the Eternal is with us.

– MV DUNLOP.[42]

Appreciating change

In learning to appreciate and develop your ability to change, it is helpful to think about how you have changed over time. You are not the same person you were ten years ago. How are you different? What were you like before? Would your present self and past self be friends if they met? What would they like and dislike about each other? How did you come to be the person you are now? Your ideals, thoughts, and opinions have changed; what has replaced the old ones and why? By reviewing the changes that have occurred, you can savor the growth and progress you have made, and appreciate the benefits the process of change has brought to your life.

When you notice how much you have changed and developed even without consciously trying, you can see how much you could grow if you made a real effort to change. It may be helpful to think about your present life in relation to the future self you will become. Will your present actions improve your life, making it rich in growth and positive experience? What will you think when you look back ten years from today? How instrumental will you have been in making the changes that have taken place? By questioning your life in this way, you can gain a clearer perspective on your motivation to change and grow.

– TARTHANG TULKU.[43]

Qualities of authentic nature

Divine love,
the heart of hearts, abounds
in every grain of being,
from atom's gleam to starry sky,
from darkest pain to brightest joy
Unceasing love kindles life –
a royal promise sealed
with the kiss of peace.

– HILDEGARDE OF BINGEN.[44]

Only when we have removed the harm in ourselves do we become truly useful to others. Through … slowly removing the unkindness and harm from ourselves, we allow our true Good Heart, the fundamental goodness and kindness that are our real nature, to shine out and become the warm climate in which our true being flowers.

– SOGYAL RINPOCHE.[45]

This Original Life is Infinite. It is good. It is filled with peace. It is of the essence of purity. It is the ultimate of intelligence. It is power. It is Law. It is in us. In that inner sanctuary of our own nature, hidden perhaps from objective gaze, 'nestles the seed, perfection.'

– EARNEST HOLMES.[46]

If I say, 'A lotus for you, a Buddha to be,' it means, 'I see clearly the Buddha nature in you.' It may be difficult for you to accept that the seed of the Buddha is in you, but we all have the capacity for faith, awakening, understanding, and awareness, and that is what is meant by Buddha nature. There is no one who does not have the capacity to be a Buddha.

– THICH NHAT HANH.[47]

Each of us possesses a soul, but we do not realize its value, as made in the image of God, therefore we fail to understand the important secret it contains.

– ST TERESA OF AVILA.[48]

Within the space of our deeper mind, everything is perfect. Despite the apparent difficulties common to our lives, here the essence of consciousness is seen to be peace.

– TARTHANG TULKU.[49]

Spiritual life – its influence, implications and rewards

Let there be many windows in your soul,
That all the glory of the universe
May beautify it. Not the narrow pane
Of one poor creed can catch the radiant rays
That shine from countless sources. Tear away
The blinds of superstition; let the light
Pour through fair windows, broad as truth itself
And as high heaven … Tune your ear
To all the worldless music of the stars
And to the voice of nature, and your heart
Shall turn to truth and goodness as the plant
Turns to the sun. A thousand unseen hands
Reach down to help you to their peace-crowned Heights
And all the forces of the firmament
Shall fortify your strength. Be not afraid
To thrust aside half-truths and grasp the whole.

– FROM TRINE.[50]

An occasional contact with God, like the proverbial grain of truth, will work wonders; but we cannot expect a complete and perfect spiritual existence simply because once in a while we remember to turn to God, or to devote a few hours to the study of spiritual books. It requires prayer without ceasing to make life a continuous experience of good.

– JOEL S GOLDSMITH.[51]

You are not to mind greatly who is for you or against you, but take good care that God is with you in everything that you do.

– THOMAS À KEMPIS.[52]

Try always to remember the eternal principles upon which life is founded and to live in harmony with them. That is the way to ensure the tranquillity, repose, calmness, peace and inner stillness that comes to all those who are in tune with the larger aspects of being.

– SILVER BIRCH.[53]

When the seeds of our actions are caring and sincere, we can know that they will bear nourishing fruit for all beings … We can only begin now, where we are, and it is this now that becomes the seed for all that lies ahead. Our responsibility, our creativity is all that is asked. With such sincere motivation, we will naturally ask wise questions and offer true care, tending what we love with a far-reaching wisdom.

– JACK KORNFIELD.[54]

Life is evolution, it is progress, a striving upwards, a developing, unfolding, extension, reaching out.

– SILVER BIRCH.[55]

Some people discover the need for honesty as well as feelings of love and compassion for themselves, for others, and for the world … they often feel a poignant respect and caring for the 'old self' that for years bore a heavy load of problems, as well as for the 'new self' that struggled courageously to come into being. Through their own hardships, many people feel a deeper connection with the suffering of others.

In addition, they might have had a mystical experience of unity with all life and realize that they cannot hurt others without hurting themselves. They might feel a deepening commitment to ease someone else's life and discover that by doing so they are also easing their own. They may become interested in using their newfound strength and insight to help others.

For many people, spirituality becomes a desirable and necessary part of life. They realize that the spiritual element has been missing from their lives. As part of their emerging process, they may have had transcendent experiences that have made them aware of previously hidden areas of existence… Whatever the route, most individuals want to stay in contact with the nourishing and inspirational dimensions they have encountered.

– CHRISTINA AND STANISLAV GROF.[56]

Inner work, spiritual work, is most effective when it proceeds hand in hand with outer work.

– STARHAWK.[57]

Universal selfhood

I am conscious that the life and intelligence within me is some part of the Universal Spirit. Therefore, I know that my mind is one with the Infinite Mind. Being one with the Infinite Mind, it is continuously guided and directed and all my actions are controlled by the Spirit within me.

I know exactly what to do in every situation. Every idea necessary to successful living is brought to my attention. The doorway to ever-increasing opportunity for self-expression is ever open before me. I am continuously meeting new and larger experiences. Every day brings more blessing and greater self-expression. I am prospered in everything I do. An abundance of good is mine today.

There is that within me which understands the Truth, which completely accepts It, which remembers freedom, expresses freedom, and anticipates freedom. There is that within me which is completely conscious of its unity with good, of its oneness with all the power there is, all the presence there is, and all the life there is. Upon this Power, Presence and Life I depend with complete certainty. I have absolute inner assurance that Divine Intelligence guides me in everything that I do.

… I know that this Presence responds to me. I know that everyone is an incarnation of God, that the living Spirit breathes through all … I recognize this Spirit and It responds to me. The Spirit within me reaches out and communes with the Spirit in everyone and everything I contact.

– ERNEST HOLMES.[58]

In the stillness we not only find our individual self, but we find our Universal Self, for the extent of every man is as vast as the Universe. The entire Universe is within each and everyone. It is only when the individuality merges away in Universality that we become boundless and timeless and experience that all is One.

– GURURAJ ANANDA.[59]

Surrendering to greater life

Father to Thee I raise my whole being,
a vessel emptied of self.
Accept, Lord, this my emptiness,
and so fill me with Thyself,
Thy Light, Thy Love, Thy Life,
that these Thy precious gifts
may radiate through me
and overflow the chalice of my heart
into the hearts of all
whom I may contact this day,
revealing unto them the beauty
of Thy Joy and Wholeness,
and the serenity of Thy Peace,
which nothing can destroy.

– THE CHALICE PRAYER.[60]

Lord, make me a channel of Thy peace that,
Where there is hatred, I may bring love;
That where there is wrong, I may bring the spirit of forgiveness;
That where there is discord, I may bring harmony;
That where there is error, I may bring truth;
That where there is doubt, I may bring faith;
That where there is despair, I may bring hope;
That where there are shadows, I may bring light;
That where there is sadness, I may bring joy;
Lord, grant that I may seek rather to comfort than to be comforted,
To understand than to be understood;
To love than to be loved.
For it is by forgetting self that one finds;
It is by forgiving that one is forgiven;
It is by dying that one awakens to eternal life.

– FRANCIS OF ASSISI.[61]

But I have spoken of great things ...
    too wonderful for me to know.
I knew of thee then only by report,
    But now I see thee with my own eyes.
Therefore I melt away ...

– Job.[62]

To forget the self is to be enlightened by all things.
To be enlightened by all things is to remove the barriers
between oneself and other.

– Dogen.[63]

Transcendence and ever-present sacredness

None of us is an independent reality. We are all parts of a whole, experiencing ourselves through our heredity, our families, our language, our race, our traditions, our customs ... So far this is on a fairly ordinary level of consciousness but we can now go to a higher level of consciousness such that we go beyond our physical consciousness and beyond our normal psychological consciousness, and then we become aware of a transcendent or transpersonal consciousness ... now we begin to discover that we ourselves are related to, and dependent on, powers and energies which are beyond us and above us.

– Bede Griffiths.[64]

And when a man sees that the God in himself is the same God in all that is, he hurts not himself by hurting others: then he goes indeed to the highest Path.

When one sees Eternity in things that pass away and Infinity in finite things, then one has pure knowledge.

– The Bhagavad Gita.[65]

It is only as you live affirmatively that you can be happy. Knowing that there is but one Spirit in which everyone lives, moves and has his being ...

– Ernest Holmes.[66]

I still remember walking down the Notting Hill main road and observing the (extremely sordid) landscape with joy and astonishment. Even the movement of the traffic had something universal and sublime in it.

— EVELYN UNDERHILL.[67]

At times I feel as if I am spread out over the landscape and inside things, and am myself living in every tree, in the splashing of the waves, in the clouds and the animals that come and go, in the procession of the seasons.

— CG JUNG.[68]

In the market, in the cloister, only God I saw;
In the valley, on the mountain, only God I saw …
I opened mine eyes and by the light of His Face around me
In all the eye discovered, only God I saw.
Like a candle I was melting in His Fire:
Amidst the flames outflashing only God I saw …
I passed away into nothingness, I vanished,
And lo, I was the All-living – only God I saw.

— BABA KUHI OF SHIRAZ.[69]

The Divine's oneness, immanence and transcendence

It is large, heavenly, of inconceivable form;
	yet it appears more minute than the minute.
It is farther than the farthest,
	yet it is here at hand;
It is right here within those who see,
	hidden within the cave of their heart.

— MUNDAKA UPANISHAD.[70]

It moves – yet it does not move
	It's far away – yet it is near at hand!
It is within this whole world – yet
	it's also outside this whole world.
When a man sees all beings
	within his very self,
	and sees his self within all beings,

It will not seek to hide from him.
When in the self of a discriminating person,
    his very self has become all beings,
What bewilderment, what sorrow can there be,
    regarding that self of him who sees this oneness.
– ISHA UPANISHAD.[71]

For God's kingdom dwells in your heart and all around you …
– JESUS (THE GOSPEL OF THOMAS).[72]

Finding truth within and allowing it to shine

Truth is within ourselves, it takes no rise
From outward things, whate'er you may believe.
There is an inner centre in us all
Where truth abides in fullness; and around
Wall upon wall the gross flesh hems it in
That perfect clear perception which is Truth.
A baffling and pervading carnal mesh
Binds all and makes all error, but to know
Rather consists in finding out a way
For the imprisoned splendour to escape
Than in achieving entry for a light
Supposed to be without.

– BROWNING.[73]

A living example of compassion

The Dalai Lama was due to attend a small reception … Among the onlookers I saw a man whom I had noticed a couple of times during the week … he had caught my attention because of his expression, one that I had frequently seen among my patients – anxious, profoundly depressed, in pain. And I thought I noticed slight repetitive involuntary movements of the musculature around his mouth …

As the Dalai Lama arrived, the crowd condensed, pressing forward to greet him … The troubled young man whom I had seen earlier, now with a somewhat bewildered expression, was crushed forward by the crowd …

As the Dalai Lama made his way through, he noticed the man ... and stopped to talk to him. The man was startled at first, and began to speak very rapidly to the Dalai Lama, who spoke a few words in return ... I saw that as the man spoke, he started to become visibly more agitated ... but instead of responding, the Dalai Lama spontaneously took the man's hand between his, patted it gently, and for several moments simply stood there silently nodding. As he held the man's hand firmly, looking into his eyes, it seemed as if he were unaware of the mass of people around him. The look of pain and agitation suddenly seemed to drain from the man's face and tears ran down his cheeks. Although the smile that surfaced and slowly spread across his features was thin, a look of comfort and gladness appeared in the man's eyes.

– HOWARD C CUTLER.[74]

Creative, Nature and Gaia conscious spirituality

We came whirling out of nothingness, scattering stars like dust – the stars made a circle and in the middle we dance ...

– RUMI.[75]

Native Americans know that all beings are part of the web of life, and we have responsibilities to this great web of interconnection. Native cultures are keenly aware that nature, the earth, the Great Spirit, and the spirit guides have taught them everything they know. It is all a gift from the divine realm through the mediation of these more familiar spirit guides who inhabit all worlds.

– WAYNE TEASDALE.[76]

There is about us, if only we have eyes to see, a creation of such spectacular profusion, spendthrift richness, and absurd detail, as to make us catch our breath in astonished wonder.

– MICHAEL MAYNE.[77]

An immersion into the deep creative powers of the universe is the most direct contact a human can have of the divine.

– THOMAS BERRY.[78]

There is a communion with God, and a communion with earth, and a communion with God through earth.

— PIERRE TEILHARD DE CHARDIN.[79]

Everyday we are engaged in a miracle which we don't even recognize: a blue sky, white clouds, green leaves, the black curious eyes of a child – our own two eyes. All is a miracle.

— THICH NHAT HANH.[80]

To me every hour of the light and dark is a miracle,
Every cubic inch of space is a miracle,
Every square yard of the surface of the earth is spread with the same,
Every foot of the interior swarms with the same.
To me the sea is a continual miracle,
The fishes that swim – the rocks – the motion of the waves – the ships with men in them,
What stranger miracles are there.

— WALT WHITMAN. [81]

We are creators at our very core. Only creating can make us happy, for in creating we tap into the deepest power of self and universe and the Divine Self. We become co-creators, that is, we create with the other forces of society, universe, and the God-self when we commit to creativity.

— MATTHEW FOX.[82]

Humankind, full of all creative possibilities, is God's work. Humankind alone is called to assist God. Humankind is called to co-create. With nature's help, humankind can set into creation all that is necessary and life-affirming.

— HILDEGARDE OF BINGEN.[83]

I do not think the measure of a civilization is how tall its buildings of concrete are, but rather how well its people have learned to relate to their environment and fellow human beings.

— SUN BEAR OF THE CHIPPEWA TRIBE.[84]

Do not denigrate anything God has created.
  All creation is simple, plain, and good.
And God is present throughout his creation.
                    – HILDEGARDE OF BINGEN.[85]

God saw everything that he had made, and indeed, it was very good.
                                    – GENESIS. [86]

Love all of God's creation, the whole earth and every grain of sand in it. Love every leaf, every ray of God's light. Love the animals, love the plants, love everything. If you love everything, you will perceive the divine mystery in things.
                    – FYODOR DOSTOYEVSKY.[87]

The idea that a God exists who created heaven and earth is truly profound. It means that the earth that we walk upon, the air that we breathe, the food that we eat, are all signs that the world is filled with mystery. Those who cherish this idea sense that everything they encounter is sacred. Nurture this idea, and it will guide the choices you make and the way you live your life.
                        – ELLEN BERNSTEIN.[88]

We are the heirs of the long evolution of Spirit. Each of us is the latest unfolding of the event of Creation. Our bodies are composed of the material that was shaped in the Big Bang. And, so, too, our spirit. The loving goodness of the universe breathes us and breathes through us, giving us life and consciousness, and the capacity to recognize and love others.
                    – RABBI MICHAEL LERNER.[89]

The first peace, which is the most important, is that which comes within the souls of people when they realize their relationship, their oneness with the universe and all its powers, and when they realize that at the centre of the universe dwells the Great Spirit and that this centre is really everywhere, it is within each of us.
                        – Black Elk.[90]

The best remedy for those who are afraid, lonely or unhappy is to go outside, somewhere where they can be quiet, alone with the heavens, nature and God. Because only then does one feel that all is as it should be and that God wishes to see people happy, amidst the simple beauty of nature... I firmly believe that nature brings solace in all troubles.

– ANNE FRANK.[91]

O life-giving sun,
off-spring of the Lord of Creation,
solitary seer of Heaven!
Spread thy Light,
and within thy blinding splendour
That I may behold thy radiant form –
That cosmic Spirit which lies at thy heart,
For I myself am That.

– ISHA UPANISHAD.[92]

Although human beings have experienced and practiced green spirituality in various forms for millions of years, I used to think it was something I invented.

That is probably not surprising. I was little more than a child – 15 years old to be exact – that morning when I first plucked up courage to defy the adults in my family and, instead of accompanying them all to church, spent Sunday morning sitting under a tree.

I have never forgotten the experience of that morning. It was early summer. The sun was shining, the campions and foxgloves were blooming pink against the green of the meadow grass and there were bumblebees buzzing around me as I snuggled into a hollow amongst the tree's roots and leaned my back against its knobbly trunk. From somewhere nearby came the scent of honeysuckle.

Across the fields, I could see the squat, stone tower of the church and I thought of my family sitting inside, on those wooden pews, singing hymns to the God in whom they had tried to persuade me to believe: a God who sat on a tall throne, somewhere above the clouds, surrounded by angels in white robes. And suddenly I knew, with a deep, inner conviction, that there was indeed a God. But it was a nameless, formless God; a God who caressed me with the dappled sunlight that filtered through the leaves, who charmed me with the scents and sounds of summer and who lived in every molecule of everything.

Whatever that God energy was, I knew that I was breathing it. And it was breathing me. It was within me and around me, in the air, the grass, the hedgerows, the birds, the clouds, my blood. It was in everything and it *was* everything, including me.

– MARIAN VAN EYK McCAIN. [93]

Quotation Sources

1. Jack Kornfield, *A Path with Heart: A Guide Through the Perils and Promises of Spiritual Life*, Rider, London, 1994, page 172.

2. Albert Einstein, from Roland Peterson's *Everyone is Right: A New Look at Comparative Religion and its Relation to Science*, DeVorss and Company, Marina del Rey, 1986, page 184.

3. Simon Parke, *The Beautiful Life: Ten New Commandments Because Life Could Be Better*, Blomsbury, London, 2007, page17.

4. John Daido Loori, from Kazuaki Tanahashi and Tensho David Schneider's *Essential Zen*, Castle Books, New Jersey, 1996, page 122.

5. Joan Cooper, *The Ancient Teaching of Yoga and the Spiritual Evolution of Man*, The Research Publishing Company, London, 1979, page 106.

6. John Welwood, from Swami Dharmananda and Santoshan's *The House of Wisdom: Yoga Spirituality of the East and West*, Mantra Books, Ropley, Hants, 2007, page 49.

7. Eknath Easwaran, *The Compassionate Universe: The Power of the Individual to Heal the Environment*, Nilgiri Press, California, 1989, pages 154–155.

8. Swami Rama, *A Call to Humanity: Revolutionary Thoughts on the Direction for Spiritual and Social Reform in our Time*, Himalayan Institute, Pennsylvania, 1988, page 122.

9. Roberto Assagioli, *Psychosynthesis: A Manual of Principles and Techniques*, Aquarian, London, 1993, page 39.

10. Myokyo-Ni (Irmgard Schloegl), *Gentling the Bull: The Ten Bull Pictures – A Spiritual Journey*, Zen Centre, London, 1990, pages 51–53.

11. CG Jung, *The Undiscovered Self*, Routledge, London, 1993, pages 6–7.

12. Hilton, *Ladder of Perfection*, from FC Happold's *Mysticism: A Study and an Anthology*, Penguin, London, 1969, page 318.

13. The Dhammapada (verses 1.1–4), translated by the Venerable Balangoda Ananda Maitreya, Parallax Press, California, 1995.

14. Adrian van Kaam, *Anger and the Gentle Life from Awakening the Heart: East/West Approaches to Psychotherapy and the Healing Relationship*, (edited by John Welwood), Shambhala, London, 1985, page 97.

15. Stephen Levine, *A Gradual Awakening: A Practical Introduction to Meditation*, Century, London, 1989, page 130.

16. Sheng-yen, from Kazuaki Tanahashi and David Schneider's *Essential Zen*, Castle Books, New Jersey, 1996, page 23.

17. *The Bhagavad Gita* (verses 2.47–48), translated by Juan Mascaro, Penguin Books, London, 1962.

18. Sri Daya Mata, *Finding the Joy Within You: Personal Counsel for God-Centred Living*, Self-Realization Fellowship, California, 1990, pages 219–220.

19. Geshe Rabten and Geshe Dhargyey, *Advice from a Spiritual Friend* (translated and edited by Brian Beresford), Wisdom, Boston, 1996, page 48.

20. Mother Teresa, *A Simple Path*, BCA, London, 1995, page 174.

21. Micah (verse 6.8), *The Green Bible: New Revised Standard Version* (with a foreword by Desmond Tutu), Harper One, New York, 2008.

22. Lao Tsu, *Tao Te Ching* (verses 29 and 63), translated by Gia-Fu and Jane English, from Bede Griffiths' *Universal Wisdom: A Journey through the Sacred Wisdom of the World*, Harper Collins, London, 1994.

23. Reshad Feild, *The Alchemy of the Heart*, Element, Dorset, page 139.

24. Tarthang Tulku, *Gestures of Balance: A Guide to Awareness, Self-healing and Meditation*, Dharma Publishing, California, 1977, pages 98–99.

25. Jesus (The Gospel of Matthew: verse 19.19), *Good News Bible*, Collins/Fontana, London, 1976.

26. The First Letter of John (verse 4.16), *The Green Bible: New Revised Standard Version* (with a foreword by Desmond Tutu), Harper One, New York, 2008.

27. Rabbi Rafael of Bershad, from Victor Gollancz' *New Year of Grace: An Anthology for Youth and Age*, Gollancz, London, 1964, page 162.

28. Robert Ellwood, *Finding Deep Joy*, A Quest Book, Illinois, 1984, page 20.

29. The Dalai Lama, *Ancient Wisdom, Modern World: Ethics for a New Millennium*, Little Brown, London, 1999, page 139.

30. Silver Birch, *More Philosophy of Silver Birch* (compiled by Tony Ortzen), Psychic Press, London, 1988, page 246.

31. Chogyam Trungpa, from Belle Valerie Gaunt and George Trevelyan's *A Tent in which to Pass a Summer Night: An Anthology for a New Age*, Coventure, London, 1977, page 39.

32. Charlotte Joko Beck, *Nothing Special: Living Zen* (edited by Steve Smith),

Harper Collins, New York, 1995, pages 57–59.

33. Sikh Morning Prayer (number 38), translated by Khushwant Singh and others, from Bede Griffiths' *Universal Wisdom: A Journey through the Sacred Wisdom of the World*, Harper Collins, London, 1994.

34. Ayya Khema, Being *Nobody, Going Nowhere: Meditations on the Buddhist Path*, Wisdom, Boston, 1987, pages 143–144.

35. The Dhammapada (verses 17.4, 12.10 and 4.7), translated by the Venerable Balangoda Ananda Maitreya, Parallax Press, California, 1995.

36. The Prophet Mohammad, from Wayne Teasdale's *The Mystic Hour: A Day Book of Interspiritual Wisdom and Devotion*, New World Library, Novato, California, 2002 page 162.

37. Thomas Merton, *Seeds of Contemplation*, Hollis and Carter, London, 1956, page 151.

38. Proverbs (verses 3.21–23), translation from the *Revised Standard Version of the Bible*, from Bede Griffiths' *Universal Wisdom: A Journey through the Sacred Wisdom of the World*, Harper Collins, London, 1994.

39. Srimad Bhagavatam, *The Wisdom of God*, translated by Swami Prabhavananda, Sri Ramakrishna Math, Mylapore, 1992, page 147.

40. A Hasidic Rabbi, from Victor Gollancz' *New Year of Grace: An Anthology for Youth and Age*, Gollancz, London, 1964, page 162.

41. Swami Paramananda, *Silence as Yoga*, Vedanta Centre, Cohasset, 1974, pages 15–16.

42. MV Dunlop, *Contemplative Meditation*, Becket Publications, Oxford, 1982, page 19.

43. Tarthang Tulku, *Skillful Means: Patterns for Success*, Dharma Publishing, California, 1991, pages 48–49.

44. Hildegarde of Bingen, from Mirabai Starr's (editor) *Hildegarde of Bingen: Devotions, prayers and Living Wisdom*, Sounds True, Boulder, Colorado, 2008, page 28.

45. Sogyal Rinpoche, *The Tibetan Book of Living and Dying*, Rider, London, 1992, pages 61–62.

46. Ernest Holmes, *The Science of Mind*, Putnam, New York, 1988, page 36.

47. Thich Nhat Hanh, *The Heart of the Buddha's Teachings: Transforming Suffering into Peace, Joy and Liberation*, Parallax Press, California, 1998, page 175.

48. St Teresa of Avila, *The Interior Castle*, Fount, London, 1995, page 169.

49. Tarthang Tulku, *Hidden Mind of Freedom*, Dharma Publishing, California, 1981, page 23.

50. Poem from Ralph Waldo Trine's *In Tune with the Infinite*, Bell, London, 1956, pages 96–97.

51. Joel S Goldsmith, *Practising the Presence of God*, Fowler, Essex, 1985, page 47.

52. Thomas à Kempis, *The Imitation of Christ*, Fount, Glasgow, 1984, page 86.

53. Silver Birch, *More Philosophy of Silver Birch* (compiled by Tony Ortzen), Psychic Press, London, 1988, page 248.

54. Jack Kornfield, *After the Ecstasy, the Laundry: How the Heart Grows Wise on the Spiritual Path*, Rider, London, 2000, pages 270–271.

55. Silver Birch, from *The Teachings of Silver Birch* (edited by AW Austen), Psychic Press, London, 1993, page 73.

56. Christina Grof and Stanislav Grof, *The Stormy Search for the Self: Understanding and Living with Spiritual Emergency*, Thorsons, London, 1995, pages 285–286.

57. Starhawk, *The Spiral Dance: A Rebirth of the Ancient Religion of the Great Goddess*, Harper San Francisco, New York, 1989, page 36 (20th anniversary edition).

58. Ernest Holmes, *How to Use the Science of Mind*, Putnam, New York, 1948, pages 58–59.

59. Gururaj Ananda, from John and Eliza Forder's *The Light Within: A Celebration of the Spirit*, Usha Publications, Dent, Cumbria, 1995, page 122.

60. *The Chalice Prayer*, from Reshad Feild's *Reason is Powerless in the Expression of Love*, Chalice Guild, Los Angeles, 1990, page 58.

61. St Francis of Assisi, *Prayer of Peace*, from Mother Teresa's *A Simple Path*, BCA, London, 1995, page 175.

62. Job (verses 42.3–6), from Robert Ellwood's *Finding Deep Joy*, A Quest Book, Illinois, 1984, page 19.

63. Dogen, from FH Cook, *Sounds of Valley Streams: Enlightenment in Dogen's Zen*, SUNY, New York, 1989, page 66.

64. Bede Griffiths, *A New Vision of Reality: Western Science, Eastern Mysticism and Christian Faith*, Fount, London, 1989, pages 263–264.

65. The Bhagavad Gita (verses 13.28 and 18.20), translated by Juan Mascaro, Penguin Books, London, 1962.

66. Ernest Holmes, *This Thing Called You*, Putnam, New York, 1985, page 145.

67. Evelyn Underhill, from Victor Gollancz' *New Year of Grace: An Anthology for Youth and Age*, Gollancz, London, 1964, page 379.

68. CG Jung, from Vivianne Crowley's *Principles of Jungian Spirituality*, Thorsons, London, 1998, page 136.

69. Baba Kuhi of Shiraz, from Sidney Spencer's *Mysticism in World Religion*, Allen and Unwin, London, 1963, page 320.

70. Mundaka Upanishad (verse 3:1.7), from *Upanisads*, translated by Patrick Olivelle, Oxford University Press, Oxford, 1996.

71. Isha Upanishad (verses 5–7), from *Upanisads*, translated by Patrick Olivelle, Oxford University Press, Oxford, 1996.

72. Jesus (The Gospel of Thomas: passage 3.3), from *The Gnostic Gospels* (a poetic translation by Alan Jacobs), Watkins, London, 2006, page 20.

73. Browning, *Paracelsus*, from Belle Valerie Gaunt and George Trevelyan's *A Tent in which to Pass a Summer Night: An Anthology for a New Age*, Coventure, London, 1977, page 118.

74. Howard C Cutler, from HH Dalai Lama and Howard C Cutler's *The Art of Happiness: A Handbook for Living*, Hodder and Stoughton, London, 1998, pages 260–261.

75. Rumi, from John and Eliza Forder's *The Light Within: A Celebration of the Spirit*, Usha Publications, Dent, Cumbria, 1995, page 16.

76. Wayne Teasdale, *The Mystic Heart: Discovering a Universal Spirituality in the World's Religions*, New World Library, Novato, California, 1999, page 186.

77. Michael Mayne, from Mark Water's (compiler) *The New Encyclopedia of Christian Quotations*, John Hunt Publishing, Alresford, Hampshire, 2000 (reprint), page 236.

78. Thomas Berry, from the foreword by Brian Swimme to Pierre Teilhard de Chardin's *The Human Phenomenon* (translated by Sarah Appleton-Weber), Sussex Academic Press, Brighton and Portland, 2003 (new edition and translation), page XV.

79. Pierre Teilhard de Chardin, *Writings in Time of War* (translated by Renà Hague), Collins, London, 1968, p. 14.

80. Thich Nhat Hanh, from Wayne's Teasdale's *The Mystic Hour: A Day Book of Interspiritual Wisdom and Devotion*, New World Library, Novato, California, 2004, page 321.

81. Walt Whitman, from *GreenSpirit: Path to a New Consciousness* (edited by Marian Van Eyk McCain), Earth Books, Ropley, Hants, 2010, page 117.

82. Matthew Fox, *Creativity: Where the Divine and the Human Meet*, Tarcher/Putnam, New York, 2002, page 28.

83. Hildegarde of Bingen, from Matthew Fox's *Original Blessing: A Primer in Creation Spirituality*, Tarcher/Putnam, New York, 1983, page 230.

84. Sun Bear of the Chippewa Tribe, from Wayne's Teasdale's *The Mystic Hour: A Day Book of Interspiritual Wisdom and Devotion*, New World Library, Novato, California, 2004, page 64.

85. Hildegarde of Bingen, from Mirabai Starr's (editor) *Hildegarde of Bingen: Devotions, prayers and Living Wisdom*, Sounds True, Boulder, Colorado, 2008, page 77.

86. Genesis (verse 1.31), *The Green Bible: New Revised Standard Version* (with a foreword by Desmond Tutu), Harper One, New York, 2008.

87. Fyodor Dostoyevsky, *The Brothers Karamazov* from Paul Harris's (editor) *The Fire of Silence and Stillness: An Anthology of Quotations for the Spiritual Journey*, Templegate Publishers, London, 1995, page 141.

88. Ellen Bernstein, *The Splendor of Creation*, A Biblical Ecology, The Pilgrim Press, Cleveland, 2005, page 2.

89. Michael Lerner, *Spirit Matters*, Walsch Books, Boston, 2000, page 42.

90. Black Elk, from Wayne Teasdale's *The Mystic Hour: A Day Book of Interspiritual Wisdom and Devotion*, New World Library, Novato, California, 2002 page 14.

91. Anne Frank, from J. Matthew Sleeth's *Teachings on Creation through the Ages* (editor), in *The Green Bible: New Revised Standard Version* (with a foreword by Desmond Tutu), Harper One, New York, 2008.

92. Isha Upanishad, from John and Eliza Forder's *The Light Within: A Celebration of the Spirit*, Usha Publications, Dent, Cumbria, 1995, page 133.

93. Marian Van Eyk McCain, from the introduction to *GreenSpirit: Path to a New Consciousness* (edited by Marian Van Eyk McCain), Earth Books, Ropley, Hants, 2010, pages 5–6.

Further Reading

Thomas Berry, with additional material by Brian Swimme, *Meditations with Thomas Berry* (selected by June Raymond).

Swami Dharmananda and Santoshan, *The House of Wisdom: Yoga Spirituality of the East and West*.

Glyn Edwards, *The Potential of Mediumship: A Collection of Essential Teachings and Exercises*.

Glyn Edwards and Santoshan, *The Spirit World in Plain English: Mediumistic and Spiritual Unfoldment*.

Matthew Fox, *Creativity: Where the Divine and the Human Meet*.

Christina Grof and Stanislav Grof, *The Stormy Search for the Self: Understanding and Living with Spiritual Emergency*.

Ernest Holmes, *This Thing Called You*.

Ursula King, *The Search for Spirituality: Our Global Quest for Meaning and Fulfilment*.

Jack Kornfield, *After the Ecstasy, the Laundry: How the Heart Grows Wise on the Spiritual Path*.

Marian Van Eyk McCain (compiled and edited by), *GreeenSpirit: Path to a New Consciousness*.

Parker J Parmer, *A Hidden Wholeness: The Journey Towards an Undivided Life.*

Ursula Roberts, *Hints on Spiritual Unfoldment.*

Santoshan, *Rivers of Green Wisdom: Exploring Christian and Yogic Earth Centred Spirituality.*

Santoshan, *Spirituality Unveiled: Awakening to Creative Life.*

Santoshan, with conversations with Glyn Edwards, *Realms of Wondrous Gifts: Psychic, Mediumistic and Miraculous Powers in the Great Wisdom Traditions.*

Wayne Teasdale, *The Mystic Heart: Discovering a Universal Spirituality in the World's Religions.*

Tarthang Tulku, *Gestures of Balance: A Guide to Awareness, Self-healing and Meditation.*

Wu Wei: *I Ching Life: Becoming your Authentic Self (Living in Harmony with Universal Law).*

Ken Wilber, *The Integral Vision: A Very Short Introduction to the Revolutionary Integral Approach to Life, God, the Universe and Everything.*

* * *

For information about Glyn Edwards and Santoshan, details about their books, CDs by Glyn Edwards and courses run by
The Gordon Higginson Fellowship,
visit www.ghfellowship.co.uk. Or see pages about them on Facebook.

The book *Spirituality Unveiled* has its own website.

For information about GreenSpirit
visit www.greenspirit.org.uk.

THE POTENTIAL OF MEDIUMSHIP
A Collection of Essential Teachings and Exercises
Glyn Edwards
Compiled and with an introduction by Santoshan

104 pages
ISBN 978-0-9569210-2-4

*eBook edition available
from Smashwords
www.smashwords.com*

Presents an inspiring collection of teachings, along with numerous essential exercises for unfolding mediumistic and spiritual gifts. In this first ever anthology of Glyn Edwards' wisdom, he shares firsthand accounts about his own mediumistic experiences and imparts profound insights that will help you to move forward with your abilities. There are chapters here for beginners and the more advanced that reveal how the spirit world can communicate with and work through us and prove survival of life after death.

'What Glyn has to share is of vital importance to all those wanting to unfold the abilities within them.'
– Mark Stone, teacher, medium and healer, Mind-Body-Spirit, Westbourne.

THE SPIRIT WORLD IN PLAIN ENGLISH
Mediumistic and Spiritual Unfoldment
Glyn Edwards and Santoshan
Foreword by Don Hills

160 pages
ISBN 78-0-9569210-0-0

The Spirit World in Plain English is a revised and updated edition of the authors' first book. In this beneficial manual, Glyn Edwards and Santoshan share practical exercises and teachings for discovering your inherent mediumistic and spiritual potential. Together, they combined their knowledge in far-reaching ways and cover numerous essentials for understanding and interacting with the ever-present world of the spirit.

'This book is more than just another book on spiritual and psychic development; it's literally the bible on development.'
– Amazon UK, customer review of first edition.

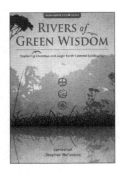

RIVERS OF GREEN WISDOM
Exploring Christian and Yogic Earth Centred Spirituality
Santoshan (Stephen Wollaston)

In *Rivers of Green Wisdom* the author shares personal reflections on Christian, Yogic and Earth centred wisdom, and unveils central teachings about the sacredness of Nature. The book covers both past and present understanding about our interdependent relationship with the natural world and how various teachers have looked for east-west fusions for deeper and more responsible living.

eBook: 16,000 words
ISBN 978-0-9552157-8-0

*Only $0.99 / £0.77 approx
Available from Amazon
and Smashwords*

'**Seldom do you find such practised clarity in revealing the wisdom of Spirit.**'
– Sky McCain, Vedantist and author of
Planet as Self: An Earthen Spirituality.

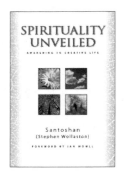

SPIRITUALITY UNVEILED
Awakening to Creative Life
Santoshan (Stephen Wollaston)
Foreword by Ian Mowll

A succinct and compelling synthesis of numerous spiritual traditions. Weaves together insights from contemporary and past masters of spirituality, along with holistic and Earth centred wisdom.

144 pages
ISBN 978-1-84694-509-0

*Amazon Kindle edition
also available*

'**Integral thinking at its best … a masterful synthesis.**'
– Marian Van Eyk McCain, editor of
GreenSpirit: Path to a New Consciousness.

CDs on Mediumistic Unfoldment by Glyn Edwards

Double CD Sets
Sitting in the Power and Sensory Awareness (2002 version)
Merging with Spirit Consciousness: Sitting in the Power and Mediumistic Unfoldment (2005 version)

All above CDs, as well as books by Glyn Edwards and Santoshan, are available from:

Mind-Body-Spirit
Tel: (01202) 267684 (outside UK: +441202 267684)
Online worldwide mail ordering service for CDs and books:
www.mindbodyspiritonline.co.uk